OPPOR

in

Sports and Fitness Careers

Ray Heitzmann

VGM Career Books

Chicago   New York   San Francisco   Lisbon   London   Madrid   Mexico City
Milan   New Delhi   San Juan   Seoul   Singapore   Sydney   Toronto

Library of Congress Cataloging-in-Publication Data

Heitzmann, William Ray.
    Opportunities in sports and fitness careers / Wm. Ray Heitzmann.
        p.   cm. — (VGM opportunities series)
    ISBN 0-658-01045-X
    1. Sports—Vocational guidance—United States.   2. Physical fitness—
Vocational guidance—United States.   3. Sports personnel—Employment—United
States.   I. Title.   II. Series.

GV734.3 .H45   2003
796'.023—dc21   2002191062

1 2 3 4 5 6 7 8 9 0   LBM/LBM   2 1 0 9 8 7 6 5 4 3

ISBN 0-658-01045-X

Interior design by Rattray Design

McGraw-Hill books are available at special quantity discounts to use as premiums and
sales promotions, or for use in corporate training programs. For more information,
please write to the Director of Special Sales, Professional Publishing, McGraw-Hill, Two
Penn Plaza, New York, NY 10121-2298. Or contact your local bookstore.

This book is printed on acid-free paper.

CONTENTS

Foreword

Survival of the fittest, for Darwin, had to do with the evolution of the species. It is, however, also a phrase that describes the state of sports and fitness in our society today. As an athlete, in addition to raw talent, you will need to develop traits that will help you excel in your chosen sport, be it a team sport or an individual one. Only the most talented and able will make it in this highly competitive world. The same can be said for one's personal physical fitness. To survive—and survive well—you will need to exercise, eat well, and pay close attention to maintaining a healthy lifestyle.

It seems obvious that both a love of sports and a desire for physical fitness are very much a part of our society. In fact, they are so important to our daily lives and so thoroughly interwoven into our culture that they offer numerous opportunities for employment to those who are attracted to them.

Consider that sports are big entertainment—sometimes an obsession—for people around the world, whether they are the athletes themselves or spectators. Millions of fans follow their favorite teams. The possibilities for a satisfying career in sports are almost limitless for those who wish to be part of the play itself as athlete, coach, umpire, sportscaster, and so forth. There are also many behind-the-scene jobs to compete for, such as sports promoter, statistician, trainer, journalist, and sports doctor.

It is also no surprise that because of the sedentary nature of many jobs in the workplace today, more and more people are looking for a way to stay fit. This is good news for those interested in helping people to achieve and maintain good levels of fitness. Many will find satisfying careers as personal trainers or nutritional consultants, as trainers for corporations and in industry, as health club owners, and more.

These and numerous other sports and fitness–related careers are examined throughout this book. For those who want to be involved, *Opportunities in Sports and Fitness Careers* is the perfect resource to start you on your way.

The Editors
VGM Career Books

ACKNOWLEDGMENTS

THE AUTHOR WOULD like to thank the many players, coaches, and other associates who have contributed to his love and knowledge of sports.

In terms of this book, the author wishes to thank specifically those listed below. Please note that the development of this book was made possible through the assistance of dozens of helpful individuals and organizations. Although many changes have taken place since the initial writing of the book, those listed here are identified by their affiliations at that time, since those connections are most relevant to the subject. In cases where individuals have changed positions, the organizations they represented are still deserving of thanks.

Barry Mano, publisher and executive editor, *Referee* magazine; Andy McGovern, sports collectible specialist, Narberth, PA; John Robinson, athletic coach and fitness specialist, San Diego; Tim McCarver, TV sports broadcaster and commentator; Deena Shelton, cameraperson, major league baseball; Vincent DiStefano, M.D., sports orthopedist, Human Performance and Sports Medicine Center, Wayne, PA; Richie Philips, attorney and sports representative; Bob Lambert, sports equipment manager, Villanova University; Henry Nichols, Ed.D., NCAA National Coordinator Men's Basketball Officials; Don Casey, Assistant Coach, Boston Celtics Professional Basketball Team, NBA; Donald Davidson, statistician and historian, U.S. Auto Club; Skippy Kingwill, basketball referee, Northern New Jersey; Otho Davis, executive director, National Athletic Trainers Association, and head athletic trainer, Philadelphia Eagles; Jim Corea, Ph.D., R.P.T., Moorestown, NJ; Larry Hanzel, athletic director (retired), North Chicago High School; James Clinkingboard, director, Educational Affairs, American Physical Therapy Association; Mary Bielinski, administrative assistant, Women's Professional Bowlers Association; Stan Gallup, executive secretary-treasurer, Golden Gloves Association of America; Vincent Francia, director of public relations and marketing, Penn National Race Course; Capt. A. J. Rubino, USNR (retired), deputy physical education officer, U.S. Naval Academy; Janet Lippincott, physical educator, coach (retired), Springside (PA) School; Canada's Sports Hall of Fame; Ronnie Barnes, New York Giants, NFL; Don Henderson, sports manager, WOGL-AM Radio, Philadelphia, PA; Tony Leodora, sports editor, *Times-Herald* newspaper, Norristown, PA; Fr. Marty Smith, OSA, Villanova University; Laura Schiller, aerobics instructor, West Chester, PA; Dick Hall, equipment manager, USMA; Joel Goodhart, professional wrestling promoter, Philadelphia, PA; Craig Miller, public relations, USA Basketball, Colorado Springs, CO; Michael Ranft, Hot Springs, AK; Andrew Clary, ATC, head athletic trainer, University of Miami (FL); Hannah Bradford, American Association of Acupuncture and Oriental Medicine; Lori Warner, public relations coordinator, National Strength and Conditioning Association, Lincoln, NE; Michael Billauer, D.C., Billauer Chiropractic Offices, Marina Del Rey, CA, and Team Physician, Men's U.S. Volleyball Olympic Team (1988); Marilee Matheny, M.S., Director of Fitness Program, Shiley Sports and Health Center of Scripps Clinic, San Diego, CA; Michael Colgan, Ph.D., Director, Colgan Institute, Encinitas, CA; Larry Shane, Athletic Department, Villanova University; Michele Sharp, women's basketball coach, Northwich University, Northfield, VT; Trudy Tappan, Ed.D., health science specialist, Richmond, VA; Dick Borkowski, Ed.D., AD, the Episcopal Academy (Merion, PA) and sports safety and law specialist; Ron Barr, host, and Larry Maxwell, producer, "Sports Byline" national radio talk show; Don Hunt, media specialist and freelance sportswriter, Philadelphia, PA; Glenn Tuckett, director of athletics, Brigham Young University; Bonnie Bekkan, editor (Social Studies School Service) and freelance writer; Larry Matthews, Ed.D., associate athletic director, Yale University; Fred Hickman, CNN Sports; Bill Brosseau, coach, Tolt H.S., Carnation, OR; Wendy Heffernan, sales associate, Foot Locker; Maureen Lewis, assistant director of public relations, Washington Bullets, NBA; Charles Watkins, Management Strategies Unlimited, Washington, DC; NY Chiropractic College; Paul Smith, sportswriter, *News-Dispatch*, Michigan City, IN; Bucky Grace, Kirkwood Fitness Center, Edgemont, PA; Howie Long, Los Angeles/Oakland Raiders, NFL, and Fox Sports; Gabe Merkin, M.D., the Sports Medicine Institute, Silver Spring, MD, and associate clinical professor, Georgetown University; Ted Aceto, Villanova University; Joe Crawford, NBA Official; Monique Berlioux, Comite International Olympique; Berny Wagner, executive director, Track and Field Association, USA; Roy Rylander, Ph.D., University of Delaware; Major Ranko Sopko, USA, administrative officer, Office of the

Director of Intercollegiate Athletics, U.S. Military Academy; James McHugh, director of procurement, U.S. Olympic Committee; Anne Moss, *Backstretch* magazine; Ed Miersch, Sports Physical Therapists, Bryn Mawr, PA; Gerry Kaplan, AD, basketball coach, O'Neil High School, New York; Ed Kershner, Tredyfrin-Easttown School District, PA; Stephanie Gaitley, women's basketball coach, St. Joseph's (PA) University; Ted Town, assistant executive director, National Collegiate Athletic Association; Ted Quendenfeld, administrative director, Temple University Center for Sports Medicine and Science; Harold J. Vanderzwagg, social studies department head, the University of Massachusetts; Marty Walsh, football and baseball official, Newark, DE; Michael Sachs, University of Maryland Medical School; Harry Wendelstadt, major league baseball umpire and baseball school director.

A special thank you is made to Kelly Green, to Mary and Rick Heitzmann, and to Villanova University.

This effort is dedicated to the young men and women I've coached and to the sports people with whom I've worked.

1

The Sports and Fitness Boom

Here's a challenge. Turn on a television set and start surfing from one channel to the next. See how many channels you can check out without encountering a ball game, fitness show, or sports-related movie. Chances are you won't get far. After all, sports and physical activity are integral parts of our culture, whether for entertainment or simply one's own physical fitness. They are so pervasive, in fact, that these combined areas provide major career potential.

Can you imagine becoming a professional athlete? Stalking the sidelines as a coach? Teaching aerobics to senior citizens? Acquiring specialized medical or health knowledge and then using it to work with athletes or fitness enthusiasts? These and other job areas provide a variety of career paths for those interested in athletics and physical fitness.

Focus on Fitness

We live in a world where life is sometimes easy, at least from the viewpoint of physical exertion. We drive a car to the mall and then ride an escalator to the second level. On the way home, we grab some food at the drive-through window of a fast-food restaurant and then eat it while watching television, using the remote control to change channels at will. But it has not always been that way.

For many thousands of years, people kept physically fit and strong through the exertion involved in finding enough to eat. The average person's physical nature was served by a life of climbing, leaping, and running in search of food. Men guarded their precious turf and obtained, kept, and protected their mates through physical means; women kept fit by working nonstop just to survive.

As the hunter-gatherer society gave way to agriculture, people spent their days planting, tilling, and harvesting crops. At the time of the Industrial Revolution in the nineteenth century, most manufacturing depended on constant physical effort. Human muscle provided at least one-third of the energy that drove the world's workshops, factories, and farms. In industrialized countries today, muscle power accounts for only a fraction of that energy expenditure. Though society has changed, altering the workplace, the human body remains the same. People still need regular, vigorous exercise to keep their bodies fit. Unfortunately, today's workplace does not provide the activity to meet our physiological needs. The result has been an increase in the incidence of a number of physical and stress-related ailments associated with a lack of proper activity.

Fortunately, people are becoming increasingly involved with improving their bodies. More and more people have begun to recognize that structured exercise and wellness programs are one of the best forms of preventive medicine. In fact, pressure to stay fit and trim is everywhere. Some insurance companies even offer rate reductions to people who participate in health fitness programs.

A major reason for the continued growth of the fitness industry is that increasing numbers of people believe that their regular workout helps prevent disease and increases longevity. Research studies strongly support the value of physical fitness to people's wellness. Also, many exercisers attest that keeping in shape helps them look and feel better. Other factors include the belief that today's adult population has more leisure time than ever before. Additionally, exercise is now an accepted part of rehabilitation programs for heart attack victims and other patients.

Of course, many people, and too many youngsters, still decline to take part in regular exercise, and unhealthy lifestyles are all too common in both adults and children. But for many others, physical fitness is a goal toward which they put real effort. Millions of North Americans swim, cycle, play basketball or volleyball, or engage in some other sport. Health club memberships continue to increase, with men and women and boys and girls of all ethnic, educational, and socioeconomic backgrounds lifting weights, running, swimming, and participating in aerobics classes.

At the same time, the growth in team sports has been phenomenal in recent decades. Virtually every high school offers a number of team sports for both boys and girls. College sports have become big business, with hundreds of intercollegiate teams competing in areas ranging from football to golf. Professional sports teams are found in every major city, and fans everywhere follow their teams—if not in person then via television, newspapers, magazines, and the Internet.

Of course, the average citizen may never play college sports or go on to a career as a pro athlete, but almost anyone can participate in some type of fitness-related activity. The benefits of exercise are widely recognized by private industry, which loses millions of dollars each year in productivity to ailments such as the common backache. Many companies sponsor active exercise programs designed to boost their employees' health as well as their productivity. Work is where most people spend a third of their weekday lives, and it is also the place where most workers sit to do their jobs. If employees benefit from a lower risk of heart attack or disability through exercise programs, the employer also gains. The firm that encourages its associates to stay fit, alert, and healthy will not only save money, but can position itself more favorably in our highly competitive world.

Companies and institutions that maintain employee fitness/wellness centers often see measurable benefits. The results of employee participation include greater employee morale; fewer days off for backaches, colds, and minor ailments; and greater employee productivity and retention. Many companies have also benefited from lower insurance premiums associated with a greater degree of "wellness" among their employees.

Health fitness has become a global industry, and more and more attention seems to be placed on the importance of a healthy lifestyle. Of course, environmental and genetic factors cannot be overlooked, but taking control can reduce or, in some instances, nullify any inherited negative traits. There's still much that can be done to lower risk for heart attacks, strokes, and hypertension. Obesity, for instance, can often be controlled through a strict medical program developed by specialists including physicians, nutritionists, and also mental-health providers, if habit and low self-esteem are significant contributing factors. Were it not for our fast-paced, pass-the-buck habits, the incidence of auto injuries and fatalities would decline. Back problems, too, one of the leading causes of "sick days" from work, would be less of a problem, and the same would hold true for eye strain, osteoporosis, and the like. Companies are more than willing (and in some cases obliged by government regulations) to provide ergonomic workstations to anyone who asks, to prevent serious back problems and repetitive stress injuries such as carpal tunnel syndrome.

With the real and critical need for intervention, the earnest desire of many millions of people for guidance, and the projected openings for rehabilitative health professionals that an aging population and technology-oriented society demand, the opportunities and the choices in health fitness are many.

In the last few decades, health clubs and suppliers of specialized health and fitness equipment have matured and, in many cases, expanded. Clubs that once offered only golf have added swimming, tennis, saunas, exercise rooms, and aerobics machines. A marked shift has taken place toward social sports in exercise facilities. For example, fitness machines and physical conditioning centers have virtually replaced boxing programs. Free weights, flat and inclined benches, and aerobics equipment such as jogging machines and stair-climbers are now a staple in even the most modest of clubs. Swimming provides the opportunity to enjoy an exercise program that gives the same muscle toning and cardiovascular benefit derived from other forms of exercise.

At one time, athletes without any real specialization were hired for positions in health clubs. Now many fitness employees have specialized training in areas such as health and physical education, sports administration, and exercise physiology. Many have bachelor's and master's degrees. The industry needs people with backgrounds in early childhood education, aquatics, physiology, kinesiology (the study of the principles of body mechanics and anatomy of human movement), and related fields. A bachelor's degree may be more of a stepping-stone in the professional careers of those in the public sector than for those in the private sector. In some areas of the public sector, a master's degree is mandatory for upper-level positions. Continuing education, either in an academic setting or through seminars and courses offered by professional associations, has become an important aspect of career advancement for many in managed health fitness.

One important side effect of industry growth is increased employment opportunity. Thousands of new jobs have opened up. Some of these are full-time positions, while others may provide work only a few nights a week. Both full-time and part-time career opportunities are expected to increase during the next decade. The explosion in technology also demands new and more sophisticated professionals. From weight trainers to aerobics instructors to recreation leaders to repetitive-stress injury therapists, the health fitness industry offers a variety of job options.

Exploring Career Options

A wide range of career opportunities is available to those with strong interests in sports or fitness. In the more traditional areas, these include careers as professional athletes, coaches, physical education teachers, and others who work for professional sport teams, colleges, high schools, and other organizations. The number of those who actually make a living as athletes is relatively small, but much greater numbers of jobs can be found in areas related to teaching, coaching, or supporting sports operations.

In the fitness area, several types of jobs have emerged. Roles as fitness instructors, managers of health clubs and fitness centers, and personal trainers represent just a few of these possibilities.

In addition, professionals such as physicians and therapists often work with people to develop exercise and nutrition programs, treat sports-related injuries, or enhance the performance of athletes, among other functions.

Before you embark on a career in sports or fitness, you should first closely examine your motivation for going into the field. Many people choose an occupation in this field because they are committed to fitness. They enjoy being physically fit and want to share this experience. Others opt for the "science" side, that is, the medical aspect of the industry, and go on to become osteopathic or chiropractic providers. A significant number of people choose the rehabilitative or therapeutic side and work as occupational, physical, and recreational therapists.

Can you see yourself going in one of these directions? Take a look at the following chapters, and you'll find an overview of the major employment possibilities in sports, fitness, and related areas.

2

MAKING IT AS A
PROFESSIONAL ATHLETE

WHAT ROLE IN our society holds more glamour than that of the professional athlete? After all, such positions offer enviable salaries, public adulation, and the opportunity not only to play, but also perhaps win championships or earn all-star status in a culture that treasures accomplishment through competition.

Anyone who dreams of becoming a professional athlete should realize that the odds against success are high, with only a relatively few participants in any sport making it to the top professional level. Fortunately, a wide variety of sports exist from which to choose. Regardless of the sport(s) chosen, it will be a long, rigorous battle that will test the physical skills and character of aspiring athletes. Only those with great desire and intensity meshed with the appropriate physical and mental skills will enter the select circle. The road is difficult, but the rewards make the effort worthwhile.

The limelight in the United States and Canada shines brightly on successful athletes. Many millions of citizens are avid sports fans, closely following one or more sports on a regular basis. Millions more are occasional viewers, taking in the Super Bowl, the Olympics, or other top events as television viewers.

The Basis for Athletic Competition

Athletics have been justified in schools and society for several reasons. Among other things, athletics provide for the physical development of young people. Although some of our citizens shorten their life expectancy because of eating habits and sedentary behavior, there exists a growing movement toward improved nutrition and physical fitness. In accordance with this recent direction by the general public, schools have begun to transmit to students the knowledge, attitudes, and skills necessary for well-being and happiness.

However, physical education specialists have neglected to secure converts to the objectives of their program. Perhaps their traditional involvement in interscholastic athletics (which likewise needs support) has drained their energies, depriving them of communicating the values of fitness and sports.

Despite the highly visible role sports teams play in our schools, there are far too many young people who have not profited from good health and fitness. A number of studies have found that excessive numbers of school-age children are overweight, sedentary, or both. Clearly schools, communities, social and professional organizations, and most importantly, families, need to give more attention to youth fitness.

On the positive side, a wave of interest in fitness has spread in America's adult community. Taking forms such as jogging, aerobics, and health club workouts, a more active orientation toward exercise and good health has begun trickling down to young people.

To some extent this re-interest in fitness is the result of what has come to be known as the "new" fitness. This orientation emphasizes a mental, spiritual, and physical approach characterized by noncompetitiveness and fun. Similarly, many young people want to preserve their bodies and remain youthful through exercise and good nutrition. Sports involvement makes a major contribution to the physical well-being of the participants.

Sports also have the potential to build character among participants. Concepts such as self-discipline, teamwork, sacrifice, and fair play can be learned and enhanced though athletic competition. Generally, with a growing number of noticeable exceptions, sports have done this. Furthermore, they provide preparation for life or life adjustment.

Any season for a given sports team often mirrors life. There are high periods when everything goes exactly right for the players and the team, such as a last-second victory or clinching a playoff spot. There are also stretches of terrible lows when nothing goes right, like fouling out of a game or committing a game-losing mistake. Life is much the same. We all may experience great happiness—a salary bonus, the birth of a child, a community award, or some recognition. Conversely, there are unhappy events—the death of a loved one, the loss of a job, even the receipt of a traffic ticket. Sports participation permits the athlete to experience adversity. The highs and lows involved in sports offer an excellent preparation for life's stresses and struggles.

Key Ingredients to a Career in Professional Sports

A career as a professional athlete is very demanding. In fact, almost lifelong preparation is necessary prior to playing pro sports.

In recent decades, a number of proven strategies have been developed to enhance athletic performance. In addition to the numerous hours on the playing field, prospective professional athletes must avail themselves of the latest developments to ensure every chance of success.

Coupled with innate ability must be a burning desire, dedication, enthusiasm, and belief in oneself. Without this, all the work in the world will not result in success.

The growing sophistication of sport science, with new inventions and procedures occurring almost daily, requires the athlete to work closely with a team or individual coach. With the odds heavily stacked against the prospect of success, the enjoyment of the means (training and conditioning) and of intermediate successes must be relished during the improbable but possible journey to employment in professional sports.

Expanded Opportunities for Women

The national and international success of women's athletics has captured the attention of all sports fans. It was not that long ago that female athletes were thought too frail to participate in sports to the extent they do today. Athletics were believed too demanding and too intense except for men.

Fortunately, the myth that women cannot engage in conditioning and training activities has quickly disappeared. Athletics expert George Colfer developed the following conclusions after reviewing the research on women and physical activity:

1. Rigorous training and athletic skill have no impact on a woman's femininity.

2. Women are perfectly capable of performing strenuous activity without any physiological impairment.
3. Active women possess a better state of health than those who are inactive.
4. Women are capable of high-level motor tasks as well as those involving endurance capacities.
5. Strength can be developed or improved in women at a higher ratio than that of men.

Colfer concluded that the training needs of women are basically the same as those of men, and there is no reason to invent unique training techniques for women. One important recent research finding was the tendency of women to have more serious knee injuries than men.

Opportunities for women in athletics have expanded greatly. At the high school level, participation among women in interscholastic sports ranges from softball and basketball to other sports such as soccer, swimming, tennis, and gymnastics. Almost all major colleges offer athletic scholarships for women. And women's professional basketball and soccer have become increasingly popular.

Basic Preparation

Although there is some debate over certain aspects of conditioning and training, most coaches and trainers agree on the importance of weight training, endurance, agility, stretching, and running for speed and cardiovascular strength. Prior to beginning any program, an athlete should review proper procedures with a knowledgeable person so as to maximize her or his efforts and avoid injury. Weight conditioning brings gains of strength and power, reduces injuries, and builds confidence. Although some opportunities exist at school gyms or health clubs, owning your personal set of free weights will offer increased opportunities to work out. You may wish to consider purchasing secondhand equipment and setting up your own gym; schools, YMCAs and YWCAs, and other groups sell their used equipment through classified ads when they purchase new equipment. Some companies offer relatively inexpensive and useful home use equipment that can aid in physical development.

"Paying the price," long a slogan in the sports world, has no greater application than in the area of physical conditioning and training. For some the price is too great, unless it is looked upon in a positive fashion. That is, the process can be as enjoyable as the product—athletic success.

Mental agility and emotional toughness are also now seen as key to athletic success. Today's sports are a sophisticated business—the person who doesn't make it in the classroom will have serious difficulties on the court or field. Perhaps this is why research tells us that athletes as a group outperform their fellow students in academics.

In the past, some athletes have obtained the stigma of dullards (and perhaps a few deserved it). Today's coaches often avoid the player who has a poor academic record because that student will have eligibility problems as well as difficulty understanding offensive and defensive systems. Today's high school, college, and pro teams not only have many plays, but the plays are often quite complicated. As sports become more complex, the mental power of athletes will need to keep pace accordingly. Remember, doing well in the classroom will contribute to your athletic performance.

On a regular, daily basis a positive mental attitude remains a must for success in athletics. Players must rise above the adversity of a particular situation to become successful. Far too often, the inexperienced player will compound a mistake by making another mistake.

The true test of a winning attitude comes late in a game when a big play is needed. Winners make those plays—they want the ball!—and they know they can do it. Losers think of excuses, prefer not to be in the game, or wish the ball would not come to them. Winning and losing become habits. Make your habit winning.

The Nutritional Advantage

The movement toward good nutrition and supplementation with vitamins, herbs, and minerals is obvious. Prospective athletes must remain particularly cautious of their food consumption. This can be a difficult task, since many Americans and Canadians neglect the importance of a balanced, healthy diet.

Prospective athletes should eat a "power breakfast"—complex carbohydrates, protein, fruit, and caffeine-free fluids, every day. This will feed your brain and body, assisting you in schoolwork and on the playing field. Unfortunately, a recent noticeable negative trend toward skipping breakfast (or eating heavily sugared cereals) has developed, seriously damaging the performance of potential athletes. Professional athletes should serve as models, even missionaries, carrying the wellness and fitness message to peers.

Several studies of school lunches found many of them lacking in some important areas and overly abundant in refined carbohydrates and fats. If your school lacks nutritious lunches, take your own. Additionally, avoid junk food, which provides little help to your physical development. Likewise, follow the suggestions of many champions who carefully watch what they eat, and don't drink alcohol or smoke.

Combining rest, relaxation, sleep, and physical training with a proper nutritional plan and a sense of self-confidence will aid you in the direction of athletic success. In fact, it's a must.

Getting Started

The variety of sports results in different methods of entering the ranks of professional athletics. Most prospective athletes begin sports at the lower levels—Little League, Pop Warner programs, YMCA/YWCA, and others—and then participate at the school they attend. Successful playing may result in a college scholarship or a contract offer. Even if this does not occur, a student can continue to play at college and/or on a local team and work to improve. Following signing a professional contract, some players enter the minor leagues; others get a direct shot at the pros. Those not making the team will often play with a semipro team and try again next season.

Other sports provide different means to make it as a pro. For examples, golf uses an apprenticeship program to train club professionals and approved tournament players; there also are PGA-tour qualifying schools. For a career in ski instruction, apprenticeship training is also required. Boxers often get started through Golden Gloves competition, and aspiring professional wrestlers may attend schools offering training for newcomers in wrestling as well as in related jobs such as ring announcer, manager, and referee.

For many professional sports, college competition provides the training ground for the next level. Virtually all professional football players move up from the college ranks, and the same is true for most professional basketball players. For others, experience in high school, supplemented by other competition at the amateur level, prepares athletes for taking a shot at the world of professional sports.

The Challenge of Breaking In

What if you don't make it into the world of professional sports? The odds are against you—about a thousand to one, or worse, in many sports! Only a few hundred players are employed at any one time in the National Basketball Association, for example, out of the thousands who play at the high school, college, and minor league levels. Don't be made overly optimistic by the appearance of new leagues and the expansion into new teams in the United States, Canada, and abroad—the numbers are still stacked against any one athlete.

In considering your future as a professional athlete, work hard to make it, but plan for your future in case you don't succeed in that direction. It may be a cliché, but it is better to have tried and not succeeded than never to have tried at all.

What if you do make it? In addition to a continuing commitment to improving yourself and giving time and service back to the society that supports you, prepare for the day your career ends. Most professional sports careers are relatively short. They are often limited by injuries, never-ending competition against other athletes, and erosion of skills as one approaches middle age.

For most players, the transition from the glory and the limelight back to "ordinary" life is difficult enough; it should not be compounded by financial problems or anxiety related to job hunting. With proper preparation, most athletes can use sports as a springboard to a fine second career. Many opportunities exist in sports; in addition, business and industry often seek out athletes for employment.

Tips for Success

In preparing for professional sports, follow these guidelines:

1. Read all you can about your sport, particularly the "how to" books and magazines.
2. Organize a plan for yourself for physical development. Keep track of your fitness activities and develop specific goals for improvement.
3. Practice, practice, practice—on your own, with others, and on organized teams. Join organizations (YMCA, YWCA, Boy Scouts, Girl Scouts, Little League, Pony League, and others). Try out for the local teams. Attend summer sports camps.
4. Build a nutritional sense. Avoid those foods that may hurt your development and choose foods and supplements that will contribute to your growth. Of course, stay away from alcohol and drugs and don't smoke.
5. Join a professional organization related to your sporting interest.
6. Demonstrate a positive mental attitude. Be sure to build your self-confidence. Become a winner, not only in sports but also in life.

3

COACHING

THE MOST VISIBLE coaches in North America are those on television guiding professional sports teams, or those from major universities, as huge crowds cheer them on. But for every head coach of the Los Angeles Lakers, Edmonton Oilers, New England Patriots, or Duke Blue Devils, thousands of others work in relative obscurity. They coach high school students, middle school children, small college teams, minor league professionals, or others. Even though they may not achieve the acclaim and financial rewards of the profession's most famous members, coaches at all levels play an important role.

Although the competition for top-level coaching jobs can be fierce, that is not necessarily the case at all levels. In fact, some observers believe that a major crisis has occurred in the coaching profession. In some areas, it has attracted insufficient numbers of people. Consequently some schools and other teams at all levels have settled for coaches with limited experience and, on occasion, little interest. This has resulted in a number of tragic situations.

Novice coaches have obtained head varsity positions without sufficient knowledge of their sport, which is normally acquired in the ranks of assistant coaches through reading, through observation of many contests, and in participation at summer camps and clinics. Sometimes rookie coaches compound this defeat with a lack of knowledge of children. The result is that many quit or are asked to leave after a couple of years and, because of this early negative experience, are lost to the profession. Of course, others continue in coaching, gradually improving their skills and records. Some move to lower levels (middle school or junior high) or become assistant coaches.

Despite attempts to reduce the emphasis upon winning, the demands upon coaches remain heavy. Players want to improve. Parents want their children to learn skills and be competitive. Administrators want to see practices, travel, games, and other events conducted in an efficient, well-organized fashion. Even with these requirements, most coaches love their job.

The opportunity to have a positive effect on young people is probably more available in coaching than in any other sports career. Thousands of coaches at all levels labor daily to develop their players to win games or events. The profession can be very rewarding, challenging, and self-fulfilling. At the same time, many days are hectic, tiring, and, on occasion, thankless. Some coaches have openly expressed their disappointment in the lack of dedication of some athletes; that is, players who have sidetracked themselves by watching television, playing computer games, or "hanging out" instead of committing themselves to self-improvement. Fortunately, the majority of athletes are more dedicated.

No one should coach young people unless he or she is familiar with and can implement the Bill of Rights for Young Athletes. Dr.

Vern Seefeldt of the Institute for the Study of Youth Sports and Dr. Rainier Martens developed it in the 1980s in response to growing concerns regarding the abuse of young athletes. It serves as an excellent guideline for youth program coaches. Some "rights" apply to coaches of high school and older players, too.

The Bill of Rights for Young Athletes
1. Right of the opportunity to participate in sports regardless of ability level.
2. Right to participate at a level that is commensurate with each child's development level.
3. Right to have qualified adult leadership.
4. Right to participate in safe, healthy environments.
5. Right of each child to share in the leadership and decision making of his or her sport participation.
6. Right to play as a child and not as an adult.
7. Right to proper preparation for participation in the sport.
8. Right to equal opportunity to strive for success.
9. Right to be treated with dignity by all involved.
10. Right to have fun through sport.

Middle School and High School Coaches

Opportunities abound for coaching young people. The expansion of minor sports such as hockey, soccer, lacrosse, field hockey, power lifting, and wrestling, and the explosion of women's sports have created a serious need for new persons to enter the profession. In fact, at some schools, programs such as freshman track and women's junior varsity volleyball have been discontinued for lack of coaching staff.

Almost all public and private schools have interscholastic athletic teams that compete against those of other schools. In some states, coaches have taken certain certification courses; in others, only certified educators may coach. However, it is possible in most public and private schools to obtain employment in a part-time situation.

Is it necessary to be a physical education teacher to serve as a coach? No. Most schools would not have enough coaches if this were a policy. In fact, many classroom teachers of various subjects enjoy the variety that their involvement with school sports permits. Many teachers believe that their involvement in after-school activities with students helps them to be more successful in the classroom.

How can you get started in coaching? As with other careers, you should begin as early as possible. (Some specific suggestions can be found later in this chapter.)

When you apply for a teaching position, indicate your willingness to serve as a sports coach. In many schools this will aid you in obtaining employment. During your employment interview, express your interest. If no opening exists, volunteer to help in scouting or other ways. Most coaches will be only too willing to have an additional assistant if the person has some knowledge, is conscientious, and can provide a service. Very few head coaches have the time necessary to extensively train or monitor an assistant's progress, so the volunteer must be a positive asset rather than a liability.

Most coaches begin their careers serving as assistant coaches, working with teams at the lower levels such as eighth grade, freshman, or junior varsity. This situation (in which the person functions as a head coach) presents a wonderful opportunity. You can gain experience working with young people while experimenting with your own offensive and defensive systems and, most importantly, learning how to teach the sport. Most successful coaches not only are knowledgeable about their sport but have the ability to transfer that knowledge to the players. Most often this ability can be developed in coaching younger players, in games played after school or on Saturday mornings. Consequently, an assignment to a team at this level should be looked upon as an opportunity for self-development; it deserves a serious commitment that will be mutually advantageous to you and to the players. Many experienced coaches believe every coach should serve an apprenticeship working with teams at the high school level to gain experience playing against a variety of offenses and defenses in various situations.

A common goal in this field is to become a head coach. Few aspire to the position of assistant coach; frequently, it is a demanding position with little recognition. However, your players will realize your ability as will the opposing coaches and your own head coach. Eventually this may result in your promotion to the position of head coach at your school or elsewhere.

Head coaches of varsity teams perform many of the same tasks as their counterparts at lower levels except that they have greater visibility, larger audiences (and frequently critics), more responsibility, and, consequently, more accountability. That is, the job is more exciting, rewarding, and glamorous, but the head coach also has greater pressure for success.

In the head coaching position there exist tremendous time pressures—more jobs need to be completed than the outsider may realize. In addition to preparing for normal teaching duties, head coaches spend numerous hours preparing to coach. Here is a partial list of typical activities:

- Discussing schedules with athletic director, school administrators, and opposing coaches
- Arranging for preseason scrimmage games
- Recruiting team managers and statisticians
- Meeting regularly with assistant coaches
- Making a schedule for scouting opponents
- Announcing tryouts
- Writing press releases for newspapers
- Planning for use of athletic facilities
- Choosing the team and selecting the starting team
- Studying scouting and analyzing opponents
- Creating a game plan
- Planning and organizing daily practices
- Clipping newspaper stories on your opponents and your team
- Inviting the players' parents to the games
- Asking knowledgeable persons to scout your team for weaknesses
- Arranging for videotaping of your team
- Encouraging players to attend summer sports camps and participate in summer sports
- Attending educational conferences for athletic coaches
- Discussing the program (and problems) with the school principal, the athletic director, and other administrators
- Writing thank-you letters to appropriate individuals
- Taking inventory and ordering new equipment

- Studying proposed rule changes
- Evaluating the success of the program, including wins and losses

If the above list looks like difficult work, you are correct; coaching is not easy. At the school level, few enter for financial reasons. Perhaps the numerous required duties lead many coaches to early retirement. It should be remembered that coaches have regular teaching duties to properly execute (such as class preparation, test correction, and course planning) as their primary obligation.

Because of those who leave coaching and the expansion of sports, many opportunities exist for coaching employment. Salaries vary with the emphasis the community places upon the sport. For example, a school district that regards football as very important may pay a coach as much as $10,000 a season; generally, coaches of major sports—football, basketball, baseball—receive salaries of around $6,000, while coaches of minor sports (tennis, wrestling, swimming) may receive around $1,500, unless there is strong local interest. Naturally this is in addition to a teaching salary. According to the U.S. Department of Labor, the median salary for K–12 teachers is approximately $42,000 a year, with some experienced teachers earning $60,000 a year or more.

An increasing number of coaches have primary employment outside the school. Their job permits the flexibility to attend practices and games; coaches in these situations need to make an extra effort to become involved in school activities (attend school fairs, school plays, and so forth) to develop relationships with administrators, faculty, and students.

At the school level, coaching, which is really an avocation, offers the opportunity to work very closely with a group of young people and have a very large impact upon their development. Many of the friendships made will be carried throughout the coach's life and will provide a continuing source of satisfaction. A coach can make a difference.

College Coaches

College coaching provides high prestige. With this increased status and recognition comes significantly greater pressure for success, as well as exposure to controversy.

At the major colleges, head coaches command excellent salaries and fringe benefits, have a number of assistant coaches and staff, and frequently have additional opportunities for extra income. Some endorse products, have their own radio or television programs, give presentations, and conduct summer sports camps.

Head coaches of minor sports and coaches at smaller colleges do not enjoy such attention and income. Some are content, not wishing to exchange their situation for the pressures of the limelight.

Often head coaches at smaller schools teach physical education courses, though some teach academic subjects or have other responsibilities on campus. They may work in the school's admissions office, direct the intramural program, or serve as assistant coach in other sports.

In addition to having coaching ability, the major college coach must have skills that enable her or him to deal with newspaper and television people. Good speaking qualities are essential, since coaches frequently speak at alumni meetings, athletic banquets, and community luncheons. Assistant coaches help with many aspects of the job, including one particularly important aspect— recruiting—and aid the head coach with her or his duties.

Much of a college coach's time is spent in convincing young persons to attend her or his college. In many situations, the coach's job relies on a consistent flow of good talent. Unfortunately, this has resulted in abuses in which players have been offered "deals" in violation of the rules that are set up by governing associations such as the National Collegiate Athletic Association and the National Association for Intercollegiate Athletics. Unfortunately, these scandals have cast a cloud over college sports.

If big-time college coaching doesn't sound attractive, don't despair. Many jobs exist at the community (junior) college and small college level. These offer the opportunity to achieve some recognition locally while deriving many of the benefits of coaching at the university level.

What opportunities exist for women? A fantastic number of situations are available at the college level for women. Just as women's opportunities have expanded in school coaching, many women's college positions now exist. In fact, several colleges have strongly emphasized women's sports, playing a major schedule of games, publicizing the team, and extensively recruiting student/athletes for scholarships. By federal law (Title IX of the Higher Education Act) women must have the same opportunities as men. All schools offer women's sports programs; most employ part-time coaches who may have other positions at the college or who derive their main income from private business. For example, a head women's coach at a college may serve as both a faculty member and coach, teaching physical education as well as coaching.

Since colleges vary in terms of size and sports emphasis, those considering a coaching career have a wide range of schools from which to choose. Consequently, you should be able to mesh your personal interests with the college of your choice.

Professional Coaches

Professional coaching is generally more pressure-packed than college coaching. At this level fewer opportunities exist, but those available do provide excellent salaries, benefits, and support staffs. If in reading this chapter you have come to the conclusion that directing athletic teams is extremely time-consuming, you are absolutely correct. Furthermore, at all levels, successful coaches work to improve themselves not only during preseason and the season itself, but throughout the entire year. This is particularly true of those managing professional teams.

At this stage, job security is most precarious; few seasons pass in which several coaches are not replaced. Persons at this level rarely remain with one team for an entire career. Coaches become more expendable than their players.

In addition to handling the normal chores common to all in this position, the technique of motivating highly paid athletes remains a challenge. Coach-player relationships are particularly important in this regard. Experienced coaches sometimes point out that coaches should not be "buddy-buddy" with adult players. They should spend significant time away from the team rather than serving as baby-sitters. This differs from lower levels in school settings, where coaches often serve in a capacity similar to that of parents.

Most professional coaches have not only assistants but also specialists such as an athletic trainer and a health and strength coach; in addition, they frequently use the services of a scouting organization to evaluate college prospects.

The professional coach serves under the team's general manager and is also responsible to the owner. In most cases, they work as a unit on decisions regarding players, such as trades and acquisitions.

Professional coaches usually come from the college ranks, although most usually gain experience as assistants on professional teams before moving to the top post. In addition to excellent salaries (most in major sports earn more than $600,000 a year and many significantly more), many opportunities exist to supplement income. Even though pro coaching openings occur often, only highly skilled and usually well-known coaches are considered for these positions. If you wish to make it to the ranks of a professional coach, years of preparation and an excellent record of success will be necessary, and this in no way guarantees the job. In some cases, experience as a professional player will help.

Considerable hoopla surrounds professional sports teams and no one can discount the glamour, the prestige, or the satisfaction of earned success. Media attention focuses no brighter anywhere in America than on winning professional coaches, nor does so little sympathy exist for a deposed loser. Fortunately, many of the skills necessary in coaching, such as organizational ability and skill in working with people, are useful in the business world. Consequently, most former professional coaches find employment in sales, public relations, and management. Others return to teaching while retaining an involvement in their sport by serving part-time as scouts. A fortunate few find careers as sports announcers.

The interest in sports shows no sign of slowing. There will be a continuing need for the few who make it to the select group designated as professional coaches.

Volunteer Coaches

Many neighborhood, church, and community teams rely upon volunteers to coach teams of young people. Little League baseball,

Babe Ruth softball, PAL, Pop Warner football, YMCA, YWCA, and many similar groups could not serve the millions of players without the free services of many coaches. Although some receive a salary, usually it is very little when the amount of time is considered. While the income may be none or little, the responsibility remains great, as most often it is here that children receive their first experience with organized sports.

In recent years, it has become fashionable to criticize the abuses and mistakes of volunteer coaches. Some of this is clearly justified—a few coaches have overemphasized winning, some need improved organizational or communication skills, and others have underemphasized the development of players—but the vast majority of volunteer coaches make a substantial contribution.

Acting as a volunteer coach can serve as an enjoyable outlet while you benefit others. Unfortunately, many take on the job with little information about the role and only superficial knowledge of the sport. In some cases, awkward solutions have occurred because of improper handling of behavior problems or an injury.

It is extremely important for any coach working with youngsters to prepare for the assignment. Volunteers should realize that youngsters will probably notice details such as how a coach dresses and talks, handles emotion, uses fair standards, and knows the rules of the sport. In addition, it must be understood that coaches can be held liable for any physical harm incurred by players in their charge.

Coaching is basically teaching, and good coaches build not only good athletes but also good citizens.

Preparing to Coach

If you're planning a career as a coach, the time to begin is now.

The American Alliance for Health, Physical Education, Recreation and Dance has cited the following list of knowledge and skills as necessary for the prospective coach. In preparing for your career, these serve as helpful guidelines:

1. An understanding of the relationship of the interscholastic program and the particular sport you are coaching to the total education program.
2. A knowledge of first aid and the safety practices and techniques pertinent to the sport you are coaching.
3. An understanding of the possibilities of legal liability as well as sound practices and preventive measures.
4. A thorough knowledge and understanding of the biological, social, moral, emotional, and spiritual values that may accrue from the activity and the best methods of bringing about these desirable outcomes.
5. A knowledge of the most acceptable principles of growth and development and their implications for the sport.
6. An understanding of the basic principles in the care and prevention of injuries together with an understanding of the proper relationship of the coach to the school or team physician.
7. An understanding of the best methods of developing and conditioning members of athletic squads.
8. The ability to speak in public to bring credit to the profession and the school and to more effectively inform the public of the educational possibilities of the sport.
9. An understanding of the basic psychological principles of motivation, stress, play, and group interaction.
10. A thorough knowledge of the fundamentals, offenses, defenses, strategies, and teaching methods involved in a

particular sport. Included will be squad organization, coaching techniques, and sound motivational procedures.
11. A knowledge and sense of responsibility for local, state, and national rules.

If you go to college to become a physical education teacher, you should achieve all of the above. Studying another program at college or not attending college means you will need to prepare yourself.

The following list offers suggestions for all those wishing to enter the ranks of the profession:

1. Participate in sports. If you are unable to compete at the varsity level, play on intramural and community teams.
2. Attend practices of several teams at various levels to observe coaches' organization and teaching techniques. This is important not only for nonathletes but also those who have participated in sports. It's easy to fall into the trap of "coaching the way you were coached."
3. Observe as many games, matches, or meets as you can. While doing so, become a student of the sport. Observe how a coach performs her or his magic or makes a mistake. For example, in basketball, how does the coach use time-outs; in hockey, how are substitutions handled; in football, what adjustments are made at halftime; or in baseball, exactly when is a relief pitcher brought in to replace the starter? Quite often the difference between a fan and one studying a game is that the fan only watches the main action (usually the ball), while the keen observer watches the behavior of the other players and the actions of the coach.

4. Study the rules and rule changes of your sport so that as coach you will be knowledgeable in using the rules for your benefit and that of your team. Strategy frequently revolves around the rules of the game, with opposing coaches working to gain an advantage.

5. Select some coaches whom you admire and use them as models. You may want to write and ask them to share some of their materials with you. Many coaches will provide information on their approaches to the sport, including specifics in areas such as practice organization and weight training. A coaching model need not have a fantastic record; many coaches are very good yet have only mediocre win-loss histories.

6. Discover what functions sports officials, scorekeepers, statisticians, and athletic directors perform at an athletic event. If you do not have athletic ability, you may wish to volunteer to serve as a manager or statistician for a team. One of the best ways to gain an excellent close-up feel of athletics is to serve as a referee, judge, or umpire. This not only enables you to practice instant recall of the rules, it also lets you gain an insight into the flow of the event. Frequently, lower-level sports teams go begging for officials. Volunteer; it will make you a better coach.

7. Investigate the off-season techniques to develop players in your sport. For example, weight training equipment and procedures, conditioning, visual enhancement, and nutrition have changed dramatically in recent years. Future coaches should stay informed about these developments. Observe athletes and their coaches in working situations during the off-season.

8. Attend professional meetings, conferences, and clinics and join the coaching associations related to your sports interest. Membership in the following organizations is strongly encouraged:

> Canadian Association of Coaches
> 141 Laurier Ave. West, Ste. 300
> Ottawa, ON
> Canada K1P 5J3
> coach.ca

> National Alliance for Youth Sports
> 2050 Vista Pkwy.
> West Palm Beach, FL 33411
> nays.org

> National Association of Basketball Coaches (College)
> 9300 W. 110th St., Ste. 640
> Overland Park, KS 66210
> nabc.ocsn.com

> National Association for Girls and Women in Sport
> 1900 Association Dr.
> Reston, VA 22091
> aahperd.org/nagws

> National High School Athletic Coaches Association
> P.O. Box 4342
> Hamden, CT 06514
> hscoaches.org

9. Develop a collection of instructional videotapes or DVDs and a library of books, articles, and clippings on coaching the sport of your interest. Also read the magazines about

coaching. Professional associations are often good sources of information about such materials.

10. Volunteer to serve as assistant coach for a team of children in your community. This will give you the experience as well as the opportunity to learn and experiment in developing your own coaching philosophy and ideas.

Coaching can be one of the most positive and wholesome careers our society has to offer. To realize these benefits, a tremendous commitment of time and energy will be needed, and the earlier you begin the better. If you think it may not be worth it, consider the following excerpt, taken from an article entitled "Thoughts about My Coach" from the magazine *Young Athlete*:

> Back in the early 1920s, when I was in the seventh grade at West Orange, New Jersey's Fairmont Middle School, I met a man who changed my whole life.
>
> His name was Lawrence Quallo, our athletic director. . . . As a youngster I was not a very good athlete, but I did my best. Then one day on the basketball court, after I had been lucky enough to score, Mr. Quallo stopped the game, came over to me and asked, "Eddie, would you like to try out for our team? . . . I think you have the makings of a good player."
>
> Thanks to Larry Quallo's influence, I went on to become a fairly good three-letter man in high school. So much did Larry inspire and guide me that, when I was in my junior year of high school, I scored over 1,000 points for the basketball team (I missed only one foul shot), scored 11 touchdowns and ran the hundred in 10 seconds flat. I tried to please Larry. My reward? He said he was more than pleased. That was enough. . . .
>
> I'm now in the Hall of Fame, but only because of Larry. He helped my dreams come true. He put a real foundation under my dreams, insuring they'd become reality. He was like a father to me, and I bless his memory every day of my life.

4

Sports Administration

ATHLETES AND COACHES may be highly visible, but their contributions to the world of sports and fitness activities might not be possible without the work of specialized managers. Men and women who hold positions in sports administration play important roles by planning, organizing, and overseeing such activities.

The explosive growth of athletics has created a serious need for individuals to manage and direct school, college, professional, and organizational programs. The latter category includes everything from the Rose Bowl to the McDonald's High School All-American Basketball Game and the Iron Man Triathlon. Competent leadership provides proper organization to each detail, resulting in success for the participant, participating schools or organizations, and, if relevant, the sponsor.

Athletic Directors

Universities, colleges, community colleges, high schools, junior highs, and middle schools (and even some elementary schools) utilize the services of an athletic director (AD). These men and women follow various career patterns, most typically with a beginning in teaching or coaching. One athletic director, for example, came to his present school as a basketball coach and physical education teacher. Upon the retirement of the previous AD, he was appointed to that position by the local board of education. In this role, he has continued with his teaching duties as physical educator while also coaching the varsity boys' basketball team. He teaches his classes in the early part of the day, leaving the afternoon free for administrative duties—scheduling, attending meetings, coordinating intramurals, and so forth. At smaller schools the AD may teach a couple of classes, while at larger schools the position often commands full-time attention.

Athletic directors at the public school level may oversee just a few sports with a minimum number of coaches, especially in smaller schools. At larger schools, their job might involve the supervision of a dozen or more teams participating in interscholastic sports.

At the college level, athletic administration might cover any number of areas. At one university, the athletic director may manage the athletic business office (including tickets and concessions); sports information; trainers and equipment managers; coaches; athletic dining hall; and stadium supervision. At a medium-sized four-year college, the range of duties might be similar, but with a smaller number of staff to supervise. At a community college, the intercollegiate sports program may consist of just five or six teams.

According to the U.S. Department of Labor, salaries range from about $40,000 to $80,000 per year for most school athletic directors, and their duties vary widely. Some college positions exceed $100,000, with a few top-level people earning much more. Normally the salary is for twelve months of work, as opposed to the ten-month commitment of most teachers.

Some professional organizations list the abilities necessary in athletic administrators. These include an understanding of:

1. The role of athletics in education and our society and the rules, regulations, policies, and procedures of the various governing bodies
2. Sound business procedures as related to athletic administration
3. Administrative problems as related to equipment and supplies
4. Problems related to facilities, both indoor and outdoor
5. School law and liability
6. The factors involved in the conduct of athletic events
7. Good public relations techniques
8. Staff relationships
9. The health aspects of athletics
10. The psychological and sociological aspects of sports
11. Marketing

Reuben Frost, former Director of Health, Physical Education, and Recreation Division, Springfield College, noted that the successful athletic director requires many important personality qualities:

1. Leadership
2. A sincere interest in youth and their development
3. A sense of humor
4. Even temperament

5. Optimism
6. A sense of justice and impartiality
7. Integrity and solidarity

Public school administrators need certification to hold their positions; this requires specialized graduate work. In addition, the following organization provides a Certified Athletic Administrator (CAA) program.

National Federation of State High School Associations
P.O. Box 690
Indianapolis, IN 46206

The AD sits at the top of the sports management triangle—a position that both challenges and rewards those who hold it.

Professional and Other Positions

In 1991, Abe Pollin, chairman of the board of the Washington Bullets, made sports history when he announced the appointment of Susan O'Malley as the president of the team. She was the first female ever to hold such a position. Pollin later commented, "I didn't realize that appointing a woman to run a team had never been done before. But she deserved it."

O'Malley, with a background in advertising, made her mark in sports while in a number of positions with the Bullets. In the forefront of sports marketing in the 1990s, she improved season ticket sales and paid attendance significantly. In addition, she negotiated expanded radio contracts for the team and financially lucrative sponsorships for courtside advertising. She moved ahead because of her understanding of the direction of sports and her ability to capitalize on her skills and knowledge for the team's benefit. Those interested in sports management must absolutely understand and implement modern sports marketing to be a success in the future.

Numerous opportunities exist for positions of administration in nonschool situations. Not all of these are top-level positions; many people serve in supportive roles directing specific aspects of a program. For example, most professional baseball teams have officials such as a director of player development, a promotions director, a director of minor league operations, and similar positions.

Most college athletic conferences have full-time administrators. Their positions often command a salary of more than $100,000 per year. Their responsibilities might include developing contracts for bowl games, negotiating television contracts, promoting their conference with the media, and helping to develop corporate and fan support.

Some conferences employ not just a commissioner, but also two or more assistant commissioners and several other persons in lower-level administrative positions. Similarly, the National Collegiate Athletic Association, under its executive director, employs a large staff including managers who work in areas such as promotion, enforcement of rules and regulations, special events, publicity, and publishing. Other organizations, such as the President's Council on Physical Fitness and Sports, employ managers to fulfill various functions.

An obvious question might be, "How does one obtain one of these positions in sports administration?" People arrive in such jobs in a variety of ways. Historically most have gone the administration route: that is, obtaining a position at a lower level and working their way to the top. Sometimes this path begins well before graduation from college. For example, a young administrator specializing in sports information may get started while still in college by working part-time in the sports information office, serving on the school newspaper, or volunteering at the school radio station. Then, after taking a low-level job after college, he or she may advance to a major administrative position.

In the future, most persons in this field will enter not only because of their on-the-job experience, but also because of their education. Administrative expertise in organization, budgeting, communications (written and oral), and human relations will still remain very important, but specific knowledge obtained in course work will increase in significance.

Education

Many colleges offer sports management and leadership programs. One of the first to do so, the University of Massachusetts offers an excellent program in sports management at the undergraduate and graduate levels. Students take courses such as the following:

Sociology of Sport and Physical Activity
History of Sport and Physical Activity
Introduction to Sport Management
College Athletics
Sport Marketing
Introduction to Sports Law
Media Relations in Sport
Public Assembly Facility Management
Seminar: Sport Broadcasting
Seminar: Writing in Sport Management
Seminar: Sport Club Management

Sport Finance and Business
Amateur Sport and the Law
Internship in Sport Management
Sport Management Policy
Professional Sports and the Law
Seminar: Sport Event Sponsorship
Sport Event Management
Seminar: International Sport Management
Seminar: Ethics in Management of Sport Organizations
Seminar: Advance Sport Marketing (Sales Strategy)
Advanced Sport Sociology
Advanced Issues in Sport Sociology
Professional Sports Industry

Graduates of the sport management program have landed positions such as:

Women's soccer coach, Fairfield University
General manager, Los Angeles Sports Arena
Office manager, Boston Garden
Executive director, University of Massachusetts Mullins
    Center
Director of broadcasting, New Jersey Nets
Account executive, Nike Incorporated
Researcher, ESPN
Vice president, Raycom Communications
Assistant sales director, Suburban Athletic Club

At Shawnee State University in Ohio, students who study sports management take courses in such topics as accounting, computer systems, finance, personnel management, management principles, marketing, and economics along with courses related more directly to sports. The latter include the following:

Philosophy of Sport
First Aid/CPR
Athlete Health Maintenance
Introduction to Sports Management
Introduction to Sport Law
Ethical Aspects of Sport
Psychology of Sport
Sociology of Sport
Sport Facility Management/Event Programming
Sport Marketing
Organization and Administration of Sport Programs
    and Athletics

The area of legal liability has increasing importance to all those in sports and specifically to those in athletic management. Knowledge of legal issues and risk management is a must. Some college courses reflect this concern, covering topics such as law and liability in athletics and basics of safety in school sports and fitness programs.

Clearly, positions in sports administration look attractive. But don't overlook the amount of work involved in such jobs. Long hours and weekend commitments are a part of a common schedule; but these people enjoy what they are doing so much they do not consider it work!

"I love my job," says Dr. Larry Matthews, an associate athletic director for sport and recreation athletics at Yale University. "We offer a wide range of sports [from a squash squad to an equestrian team]; similarly, our intramural program provides opportunities from aerobics to women's flag football," he says.

Clearly, you must enjoy working with young people to serve in school sports management; in addition, you should try for employment at a school or college that emphasizes your sport(s). If you love wrestling, you should apply for positions at schools that have a wrestling tradition.

If sports management interests you, consult your school counselor for college programs and participate in sports in some capacity (player, student manager/trainer, or school paper sportswriter). Whenever possible, observe athletic administrators in their roles. Study sporting events from the perspective of management (scheduling and paying of the officials). Volunteer to assist at these games and contests. The following materials provide valuable information for present and future sports management personnel.

American Sport Education Program
1607 N. Market St.
Champaign, IL 61825
asep.com
(ASEP courses for administrators)

Athletic Administration: A Comprehensive Guide
National Interscholastic Athletic Administrators Association
P.O. Box 690
Indianapolis, IN 46206
nfhs.org

Athletic Business (periodical)
4130 Lien Rd.
Madison, WI 53704
athleticbusiness.com

Athletic Director's Survival Guide
Prentice Hall Professional Technical Reference
Upper Saddle River, NJ 07458
phptr.com

Strategies (periodical)
American Alliance for Health, Physical Education, Recreation
and Dance
1900 Association Dr.
Reston, VA 20191
(state affiliates provide information also; student
memberships exist)

5

Sports Officiating

ALMOST EVERY SPORTS lover relishes being close to the game—down on the court, out on the field—but only a few can do it as an official. This career clearly tests the character, energy, knowledge, skills, and fitness of the participants as they make split-second decisions.

For many years, officiating was considered a thankless job, where the official withstood verbal barrages and occasionally physical abuse from the coach, players, and crowds. More recently, a growing respect has been noticeable at all levels for the men and women who make the game work by enforcing the rules. This has probably occurred because of a growing militancy on the part of the officials, an increase in their skills, and a realization of their importance and dedication by the public.

A strong movement exists within the profession of officiating to upgrade the performance quality of the officials on a continuous basis. Consequently at the college level, mandatory development programs exist in many Division I sports; and at the school level, many states now require attendance at a training camp/clinic to be eligible to work a state tournament game. For example, some states require all high school baseball umpires to attend at least one special training session if they wish to receive consideration to officiate in the state's tournament games. As this movement spreads to additional states, officials may gain a further increase in status, salaries will rise, and the career will attract additional potential members.

Although full-time officiating jobs represent the pinnacle of the profession, more than 90 percent of all officials serve on a part-time basis. They work mainly with schools, colleges, semiprofessional teams, or recreation leagues.

For a typical high school official, a day's duties may consist of working in an area largely unrelated to officiating, such as teaching elementary school, working in a recreation department, or even serving as a salesperson. Then at the end of the day, he or she travels to a stadium, gym, or playing field and puts in time as a referee or umpire. Officiating assignments may vary by sport or season, such as men's and women's basketball and volleyball games in the winter and softball or baseball in the spring and summer. Although many officials earn their livelihood as educators, others own their own businesses or work flexible hours in other career areas so as to be available for afternoon sporting events.

Most view the profession as an avocation, but only a select few make it to the circle of full-time professional officials. These individuals normally "pay their dues" by obtaining several years of experience at the lower levels, such as high school, college, and the minor leagues. Richie Powers, in his classic book *Overtime* (published by Ballantine), provided an excellent look at the life of a professional basketball official in the National Basketball Association. He stated:

I'm usually quick with the whistle and even quicker with my thumb, in the area of technical fouls, but I set a record tonight by calling my first technical of the season less than two minutes into the game. Manny (Sokol) had called a foul against Phil Chenier of the Bullets. Instead of rolling the ball to Manny, or at least bouncing it toward him, Chenier held it defiantly, glaring in Manny's direction. Then he flipped the ball out of bounds. Tweet! I hit him with a technical foul for unsportsmanlike conduct . . . Listen, I call technical fouls in an attempt to maintain control of the game.

Obviously, the emotional control of officials is tested many times in each game. Maintaining a disciplined and evenhanded demeanor is a basic requirement for most officiating tasks.

Officiating Guidelines

Veteran official Tom Kline said that using humor "can diffuse a potentially volatile situation as a reminder that we are involved in a game that should be kept in proper perspective." In addition, potential officials might keep in mind the following guidelines, published by *Referee* magazine.*

- **Be competitive**. The players give maximum effort, so should you. Tell yourself, "I'm not going to let this game get away from me. I am better than that." You are hired to make the calls that control the game—make them!
- **Have your head on right**. Don't think your striped shirt grants you immunity from having to take a little criticism.

---

*Reprinted with permission from *Referee* magazine. For subscription information contact *Referee* magazine. Its address is listed later in this chapter.

It's part of officiating. Plan on it. Successful officials know how much to take. Ask one when you get the chance.

- **Don't be a tough guy.** If a coach is on your back but not enough to warrant a penalty, then stay away from him (or her). This is especially true during time-outs. Standing near an unhappy coach just to "show him" will only lead to further tensions. Some officials develop irritating characteristics. Don't be one of them.
- **Get into the flow of the game.** Each game is different. Good officials can feel this difference. Concentrate on the reactions of the players. Take note if the tempo of the game changes. A ragged game calls for a different style of officiating from a smooth one.
- **Don't bark.** If you don't like to be shouted at, don't shout at someone else. Be firm but with a normal, relaxed voice. This technique will do wonders in helping you to reduce the pressure. Shouting indicates a loss of control—not only of oneself, but also of the game.
- **Show confidence.** Cockiness has absolutely no place in officiating. You want to exude confidence. Your presence should command respect from the participants. As in any walk of life, appearance, manner, and voice determine how you are accepted. Try to present the proper image.
- **Forget the fans.** As a group, fans exhibit three characteristics: ignorance of the rules, highly emotional partisanship, and delight in antagonizing the officials. Accepting this fact will help you ignore the fans, unless they interrupt the game or stand in the way of you doing your job.
- **Answer reasonable questions.** Treat coaches and players in a courteous way. If they ask you a question reasonably, answer them in a polite way. If they get your ear by saying,

"Hey, Ref, I want to ask you something," and then start telling you off, interrupt and remind them of the reason for the discussion. Be firm, but relaxed.

- **Choose your words wisely.** Don't obviously threaten a coach or players. This will only put them on the defensive. More importantly, you will have placed yourself on the spot. If you feel a situation is serious enough to warrant a threat, then it is serious enough to penalize without invoking a threat. Obviously some things you say will be a form of threat, but using the proper words can make it subtle.

- **Stay cool.** Your purpose is to establish a calm environment for the game. Fans, coaches, and players alike easily spot nervous or edgy officials. Avoid chewing gum, pacing around, or displaying a wide range of emotions prior to or during a game; this will serve to make you seem vulnerable to the pressure.

These suggestions, generally applicable to officiating at all levels, may need slight modification in special situations. However, as a whole they provide excellent guidelines. In general, establishing and maintaining rapport with coaches and players alike will help the official avoid many potentially difficult situations. These can vary from the aggressive behavior of some coaches to challenges by rowdy crowds.

At this point you may ask, "If officiating is so demanding in terms of working conditions, why do people do it?" The answers are many. Common motivations include the chance to earn extra income, the opportunity to remain close to athletics in some capacity, and the potential to enjoy a position of some status and power. If you think this career looks promising for you, make plans to begin.

Starting Points

What kind of person makes a good sports official? Of course knowledge of sports is essential, as is the ability to understand and recall the various rules and regulations in a given sport. In addition, it helps to possess certain personality characteristics. These include tolerance, self-confidence, and the ability to make decisions under stress. There is one way to see if you possess such traits: give officiating a try.

Volunteer to officiate intramurals at a school or college, in a church or synagogue league in your neighborhood, or in a community recreation program. Such involvement will help both you and the league. Some youth leagues and intramural programs even will provide salaries, but your greatest benefit will be experience. In addition, officiating is an excellent way to really understand a sport; it will give you a better appreciation of the total game as well as a working knowledge of the rules. This serves as a valuable background for a career as a professional athlete or coach.

If you become seriously interested, it's useful to remember that officiating parallels coaching in many respects. That is, novices work with younger players at the lower level. So following approval, you will usually work games at the junior high school and the junior varsity level. To receive initial status, it will be necessary to pass a written examination in the sport or sports of your choice and to join the state association and the local chapter.

Many leagues go begging for officials. Who's going to ref college intramurals? Who's going to ref the winter Optimist basketball league? Who's going to ref the neighborhood girls' softball teams? Many leagues cannot attract or afford certified officials; consequently, this provides you opportunities. More and more the door is wide open for women as well as men.

During the probationary period, usually a couple of years, the newcomer will come under the observation of senior officials for evaluation. They will look for a good working knowledge of the game combined with several abilities; for example, how does he or she perform in a stressful situation? As new officials improve their skills they will be asked to work more games and be promoted to higher-level games, perhaps even an important tournament or championship event. Naturally, salaries improve with the level officiated and with geographic location; most have improved significantly in recent years.

Some officials will want to move on to the college level. This will involve joining another association, taking a test, and proving oneself again. College officials receive excellent per-game salaries, and most conferences also pay travel expenses.

The requirements for an official at one major college conference include the following:

Applicants for officials' positions should be in good physical condition and able to pass an exam. These characteristics and three ability references must be submitted and, while a high school diploma is necessary, a college degree is preferred. In addition, the person must have employment and residence in close proximity to the conference. The candidate's job has to permit flexibility so as to be free for travel and games. Some background as a player is desirable, but the officiating experience must include eight to ten years at the high school level; four to ten years at the community college and/or four-year college level; and approximately four years in a compatible conference.

If these criteria appear too demanding, remember that most positions will not be this difficult to obtain. The above requirements represent a special situation for one of the nation's premier conferences.

Officiating Schools

Although a study of the readership of *Referee* magazine indicated that most officials became introduced to their profession by a friend or through participation in sports, many future officials will probably enter their careers as a result of attendance at a school. Naturally, the officials associations will provide a training program for their new recruits; the schools, however, represent an in-depth concentrated approach to learning the official's art. Some master officials conduct annual conferences for officials. These clinics (often consisting of two-day meetings) exist for officials of all levels who wish to improve their skills.

The following serve as typical examples of the schools available. The Harry Wendelstedt School for Umpires, as its name implies, educates baseball umpires. The specific purpose is to supply supervised training for young people to qualify for umpire positions in professional, college, high school, semipro, and sandlot baseball. The school, which meets for six weeks, runs from directly after the New Year's holiday until early February. The program follows this schedule: Classes begin at 8:30 in the morning with a ninety-minute session that explains and tests the student's knowledge of the rules and situations that actually confront umpires. At 10:30 the class reports to the playing fields. A program of exercises and conditioning takes place. Following this, a series of practice drills takes place to teach proper mechanics—stance, voice control, positions, and others. Each student receives instruction and practice in all phases of umpiring. After the completion of the first ten days of school, the late afternoons, 3:30 until 6:00, are spent working high school and college games. Naturally no jobs are promised, but many, many of the graduates have entered the profession at all levels. Each year, some exceptional students do receive appointments directly after finishing the school, and others are called at a later date. This school has trained the majority of the men in blue working in the majors today. If this sounds interesting, write to the following address for additional information:

Harry Wendelstedt School for Umpires
88 South Street Andrews Dr.
Ormond Beach, FL 31074
daytonatrophy.com/umpireschool

Another umpiring school is the Jim Evans Academy of Professional Umpiring in Kissimmee, Florida. For information contact the school at its year-round address:

Jim Evans Academy of Professional Umpiring
12741 Research Blvd., Ste. 401
Austin, TX 78759
umpireacademy.com

For information about other schools, camps, and training opportunities in various sports, check with working officials in your area, nearby college athletic departments, or professional sports officials in your region. The Internet can also be a source of helpful information. For example, more than twenty schools and camps in the United States and Canada on basketball officiating are listed at dmoz.org/Sports/Basketball/Officiating/Associations.

Once the right credentials have been obtained, opportunities exist in all areas for officials, but particularly in women's sports and certain minor sports. Salaries vary. An official may earn $40 or $60 per game for high school major varsity sports and significantly more at the college level. Tournaments and championship games command more money. Professional salaries will vary with the sport and the number of games. Baseball umpires average more than $100,000 per year for their full-time jobs, and boxing officials receive a per-event salary. Depending on their level, minor league baseball umpires can expect to earn $1,900 to $3,400 per month for full season games.

The expansion of sports at all levels and the growth of women's participation guarantee opportunities for new officials. In addition, retirements of existing officials will lead to significant numbers of openings.

Preparing for a Future in Officiating

First, read about your future profession—subscribe to *Referee* magazine; it contains excellent information, updates, current happenings, profiles of successful officials, and suggestions for improvements. For a subscription write:

Referee Magazine
P.O. Box 161
Franksville, WI 53126
(262) 632-8855
referee.com

Also read the study books on officiating, such as those available from *Referee* magazine, including *Baseball Umpires Guidebook, 19 Smart Moves for the Basketball Official, Soccer Officials Guidebook, Football Officials Guide,* and *Smart Football Officiating.* Other helpful books include:

- *Psychology of Officiating,* by Robert Weinburg (Human Kinetics, 1995).

- *Standing the Gaff: The Life and Hard Times of a Minor League Umpire*, by Harry "Steamboat" Johnson (University of Nebraska Press, 1994).
- *101 Tips for Youth Sports Officials*, by Bob Still and Jeffrey Stern (Referee Enterprises, 2000).

Especially inspiring are "inside stories" such as Eric Gregg's book, *Working the Plate: The Eric Gregg Story* (William Morrow, 1990), which provides excellent insight into the life of an African-American umpire's rise from the minors to the big leagues. His comments apply to all officials regardless of race. Similarly, Pam Postema's *You Got to Have Balls to Make It in This League* (Simon and Schuster, 1992) details a woman's experience in the baseball world trying to make it to the major leagues.

If officiating represents a potential career for you, pursue these suggestions:

1. As suggested earlier, volunteer to officiate wherever you can find an opportunity. Many exist. What you don't earn in salary you will gain in experience.
2. Study and master the rules for your sport. Stay aware of recent changes, interpretations, and emphases.
3. Participate to the extent you are able in the sport of your interest.
4. Work to develop the personality traits of an official, such as independence, maturity, self-confidence, and a high moral character.
5. Study your sport and its officials. Use your imagination and make the calls. It will be good practice.
6. Check out websites of major sports organizations. For example, major league baseball (mlb.com) offers a Web

page on "How to Become an Umpire." Take a look also at the National Association of Sports Officials website at naso.org for valuable information on how to get started.

Remember, despite the criticism officials too frequently get, most fans, players, and coaches greatly appreciate their role. This point was made by Ron Luciano, former major league baseball umpire in his enjoyable *The Fall of the Roman Umpire* (Bantam, 1986). "Without skilled umpires, I knew, the game could not exist. Oh, players were important, I accepted that, but there were plenty of players—too many players as far as some umpires were concerned. But there were only a select few people with the knowledge and judgment required to control a major-league game."

6

Sports Journalism

How about controlling the airwaves with snappy sports talk, clever interviews, and colorful caller comments? No, not as an announcer or color commentator, but as a producer!

A whole world of activity exists behind the scenes of sports shows—scheduling guests, screening calls, scripting commercials, arranging traffic and weather reports, updating news, and other related activities. Producers handle these functions. And that's just one job area category within this field.

Sports talk radio employs a variety of personnel to support the show—sales executives, accountants, engineers, producers, executive producers, and, of course, the host. Some hosts perform more than one function. For example, one professional in this area might works as a general assignment news reporter on weekdays, but then on weekends take to the airwaves with sports. Another might write sports for a newspaper full-time and do a TV sports talk show once a week.

Radio also provides an assortment of opportunities. Show hosts vary from "in-your-face talk" to "mild commentary" by the broadcaster about the performance of local teams and players, interviews with interesting sports personalities, and telephone calls from listeners. This job requires excellent knowledge of many sports, as the broadcaster frequently is "on the spot," and it is only for persons who really love athletics. Many off-time days will find broadcasters attending games, press conferences, station promotions, and team practices. In addition to their shows, some handle sports news for their station.

Some broadcasters have college backgrounds, but others do not; many worked as print journalists and sports announcers; some did games on cable, played or coached athletics, or worked at stations and got a break. Regardless of the route taken, when the bell rang they were ready.

Newspaper Sportswriters

Almost every newspaper includes a sports section. Even smaller papers will generally include sports coverage as a part of their operations.

For many years some of the finest journalism has been found on the sports pages of America's papers. It is here that lively, fast-paced action writing appears. The size, circulation, and location of a paper will determine to a large degree the activities of the sportswriters. The sports department of small-town newspapers normally has an editor and another writer and perhaps two part-timers who cover weekend events. Such a paper will rely upon the electronic services for major, out-of-town stories.

A large city daily may have a staff of ten; several of these will have a particular specialty such as golf, football, boxing, or the high school scene. In addition to writing several articles a week related to their expertise, these persons would cover other events during the season as well.

Frequently reporters work unusual hours and days. Those who are employed by a morning newspaper may work late afternoon and evening hours, usually five days a week, including Saturday and Sunday, if there's a Sunday edition. They would then have two weekdays off. Major papers will send a reporter along with the team to cover out-of-town stories; while this sounds glamorous, it frequently is time-consuming and hectic. Following the event, the writer will use his or her notes to prepare the article, looking for a particular angle or interesting aspect to highlight for reader appeal. The writer sends in the completed article and finally gets to sleep, usually about 2:00 A.M.

Preparing for a Sportswriting Career

Opportunities exist with many school and college newspapers to begin your career. If a vacancy does not exist in sports, take a position writing news; it will help you build your craft of writing and will aid you to make a switch to sports when an opening occurs.

There may be a lot of free tickets given out, but newspapers are notorious for paying mediocre salaries to their professionals, and smaller papers pay even less. Of course, it's possible that you will gain a reputation and your own column and a substantial income. "Having a column" means your work appears regularly in the same location in the paper, usually under your photograph. In terms of your career, it marks your success as a sportswriter. Your column would be commentary, mixed with reporting.

Many writers also produce books as a sideline. This serves as a creative outlet for their talents as well as an additional source of income. A considerable market exists for sports books, and publishers look for manuscripts from newspaper people. Likewise, sports magazines look for feature articles; this is an excellent source of income for the writer and permits him or her to gain a wider audience.

At one time, reporters began their careers as copy aides helping around the office by performing clerical tasks. Having proven themselves reliable, they might have been asked to join the staff as cub reporters, which would involve small, unspectacular assignments eventually leading up to important tasks. Today, few start this way. Most attend college and pursue course work in the department or school of journalism or mass communication. Ask a school counselor for information on colleges with programs in these areas. If you plan such a career, include several courses in writing; grammar skills will be a necessity. You should also consider a strong background in the humanities and using your free electives to take sports courses from the physical education program. Courses in photography will increase your chances of obtaining a job, particularly with smaller papers.

Some working sportswriters suggest that while you're in college you make a strong effort to land a summer or part-time job with a local newspaper. Serving on a student newspaper can also be helpful. In either case, constant news experience is the key to becoming a good sportswriter. Such experience will greatly enhance your ability to obtain a full-time position following graduation.

In recent years, the expansion of television, radio, and Web-related coverage of sporting events has resulted in a modification of newspaper coverage. A decline in straight factual reporting and an increase in features have occurred. The reader wants to know not only what happened, but such additional information as the condition of the injured player, who might be traded, and the likelihood of success against the next opponent. Some outstanding features have resulted from careful excellent investigative research revealing serious abuses in sports. However, most are interviews with an athlete answering a series of questions about an aspect of her or his career.

Despite its outward appearance, the life of a newspaper person has its lonely side. In fact, one observer found that "creative loneliness" is an important characteristic of successful writers. After the big game or press conference, the hard work of writing, editing, and rewriting must be completed—and prior to the deadline!

A newspaper writer at this point in time has a very special obligation to society to remain vigilant for excesses that may destroy sports. Too frequently athletes, coaches, and administrators have engaged for personal benefit in conduct detrimental to their own profession. Coaches have forced injured players to participate; athletic directors have condoned illegal recruiting; players have put their own importance above that of their team and their sport; youth league managers have played only to win; and coaches have publicly abused players for mistakes. Even parents pressure their children unduly to be superstars. It is here that the writer can make an important contribution.

The number of big-city papers has diminished in recent years; however, many papers have expanded and many others have started in new locations. Opportunities exist for well-prepared and knowledgeable candidates. Although this field can be glamorous, potential writers should realize it is very hard work. Even the writers considered the best in the country would tell you that it took years and years of dedicated effort to develop their craft.

Sportscasters

"I broke in by going to magazines such as *Sports Illustrated* and *Women's Sports*. I said to myself, 'Even if I'm not on the air, I can research and write articles.' For broadcast journalism you need to look into the history of events and understand personalities," says Donna de Varona, a radio sports commentator.

De Varona points out that, as with all other sports careers, you must pay the price; that is, earn the position that you wish to attain. She became a household word through writing and broadcast success.

The sports world gives as much attention to well-known sports personalities from the broadcast media as they do some athletes. The glamour usually surrounds the television announcers who have great visibility and excellent salaries.

Often the hard work and time-consuming nature of "showbiz" sports careers goes unnoticed. Consider a day in the life of former CNN Sports newscaster Fred Hickman on an "easy" day!

The day for me usually begins about 7:00 A.M. That's when I kiss my wife good morning and take the dog out to pick up the newspapers. I read several to begin preparation . . . the *Atlanta Constitution*, the *Chicago Tribune*, the *New York Times*, the *Los Angeles Times*, and *USA Today*.

I scan all of these thoroughly to give myself a feel of the current sports affairs and the different slants journalists are taking on them around the country.

Then it's telephone time. I check in with my office. I check in with different sources I have about the nation. In my early days in news, they were called the "beat calls," and I've never quite lost the habit. I think it's a good one.

I can hit CNN about 4:30 P.M., which is when we have our nightly production meeting. My co-anchor and I sit in with the show producers and assignment editor to get up to speed on what's happening and lay out the 11:00 P.M. broadcast. This is generally a thirty-minute affair.

Next it's off to makeup about 5:00 before heading back down to the computer to get started on the on-air promos. I tape two per evening to be aired on all the Turner Networks.

I then am ready to begin writing the show by 7:15. I get the readers out of the way as soon as possible so as to be able to devote as much time to watching the games I'm responsible for covering that night.

I am also still working the telephones, the wires, etc., standing by for breaking news and how the breaking news will change the show.

I am finished writing by 10:30 but . . . unfortunately, the games don't always want to end just on time. This means the show is transforming all the time, even while we are on the air.

At 11:30, the red light goes off and I head home to mama.

But, in parting, may I say there is no such thing as a "typical" day in my working life. It's always different, always challenging, and always a blessing to feel the satisfaction I get from performing my task. Wouldn't trade it for a million bucks.

Television announcers earn the best salaries and enjoy the greatest exposure to the public. They may be employed by a team, a station, or both. Some serve as the sports person on the station's news program. As such, they cover many areas necessitating a good knowledge at least of the major sports. Although they may appear on the show only twice a day for four or five minutes, they spend most of the day preparing for their air time. Often this involves attending press conferences, interviewing players, and covering games. It's an exciting life that brings the sportscaster in close contact with the athletic world. Many try their hand at automobile racing, playing quarterback (in practice), and pitching batting practice as a promotion. This occurs to increase viewer interest and to expand the announcer's credibility as being knowledgeable about sports. In addition to very good speaking ability, writing skills are also essential, since sportscasters compose the information they announce.

Closely related to the television news position is that of the radio newscaster. Some major stations in larger cities will employ a full-time specialist in this area; however, at smaller stations the sports person will handle other news stories as needed and may even serve as a part-time salesperson, obtaining commercials to be aired on the station.

Sports announcers have captured the attention of the American public, whether it's during a Monday night football game, the NBA playoffs, or the winter Olympics. Clearly enjoying one of the glamour careers within the sports industry, they generally fall into two categories: play-by-play or color specialists. The former generally explains each play as it occurs and its relationship to the overall game. The color person, usually a former player, provides insights to certain techniques and strategies the coach or athlete may employ; he or she will often provide amusing anecdotes about players. Most recently there has been an attempt to carefully put together a team of announcers who will complement each other's abilities and contribute to the listener's enjoyment of the game. The staff spends many hours preparing for a game or event. Reading of players' backgrounds, talking with coaching staffs, and meeting with public relations specialists help in this regard.

How do you get started in this field? Knowledge of sports and an excellent or unique speaking voice form a very important prerequisite for the sportscaster's career. Often physical attractiveness also looms important for the television positions. To prepare for a career in this area, it is useful to take many of the same courses suggested for newspaper and public relations careers. These include courses in writing, public speaking, sport studies, and physical education. Similarly, try to become involved in sports at some level of activity. Also, obtain a position writing for a school paper or a community newsletter or working for a college radio station. If you do not attend college (or even if you do), consider attending a technical school designed for those seeking radio and television careers. These centers offer short, intensive courses and aid in placement in jobs. If you wish additional information, contact the following organization with your request for a list of these schools in your area:

Career College Association
10 G St. NE, Ste. 750
Washington, DC 20002

One option is to pursue courses offered by the Connecticut School of Broadcasting, which is located in several states. This intense program offers courses in areas such as announcing, studio operations, commercial interpretation, broadcast journalism, copy writing, audio production, and sports. Schools such as CSB provide lectures, hands-on training and practice, and career advisement for students. Contact the school at:

Connecticut School of Broadcasting
Media Park, Birdseye Rd.
Farmington, CT 06032
800tvradio.com

Hofstra University is another school providing instruction in this area through its Sports Broadcasting Institute. Normally offered over a two-week period in the summer, the institute's courses are taught by practicing sports broadcasters and executives. They emphasize the development of skills in television and radio reporting, anchoring, and play-by-play and sports commentary. Additional instruction covers radio broadcasting and multimedia applications such as Internet sportswriting and reporting.

During the sessions, students listen to guest speakers, complete in-class remote assignments, and complete a number of practice sessions. Upon course completion, each student leaves with a television and radio audition tape.

For more information contact:

University College for Continuing Education
250 Hofstra University
Hempstead, NY 11549-2500
hofstra.edu

Once you have obtained the necessary education, a smart approach is to follow the suggestion of Keith Jackson of ABC Sports, who says that if you want to be a television sportscaster, begin where you are comfortable. You shouldn't be so eager to run for the big city when the smaller community affords the better learning experience.

Many, many opportunities exist at the thousands of radio and hundreds of television stations in North America. Here the novice hones her or his skills and learns the art of the professional. Some individuals so enjoy their jobs in small towns and cities that they stay and make it a career. Others will use this background as a springboard to the "big time."

For additional information on sports journalism contact:

National Association of Broadcasters
1771 N Street NW
Washington, DC 20036
nab.org

National Sportscasters and Sportswriters Association
P.O. Drawer 559
Salisbury, NC 28144
sgma.com

7

TEACHING

THE ELEMENTS OF sports and fitness are multifaceted. Anyone can be a sports fan, but it takes special knowledge to teach relevant information about athletics and physical fitness to children and adults. Teachers in these areas can enjoy solid career potential.

In some regions of the United States and Canada, demand for teachers is limited and competition for existing positions is great. In others, growing school enrollments and teacher retirements are leading to increased job openings. In either case, some still see this as an attractive profession because of the chance to work with young people and to teach them physical education skills. Often coaches come from the ranks of physical education teachers, so this, too, looms as one of the attractions of the profession.

Teaching Physical Education

Almost every school includes physical education as a standard part of its curriculum. In general, PE programs and courses follow state-mandated guidelines. For instance, physical education goals established by the state of New Jersey for its public school students include:

- All students will learn health promotion and disease prevention concepts and health-enhancing behaviors.
- All students will learn health-enhancing personal, interpersonal, and life skills.
- All students will learn the physical, mental, emotional, and social effects of the use and abuse of alcohol, tobacco, and other drugs.
- All students will learn the biological, social, cultural, and psychological aspects of human sexuality and family life.
- All students will learn and apply movement concepts and skills that foster participation in physical activities throughout life.
- All students will learn and apply health-related fitness concepts.

In recent years, many states and school districts have made curriculum changes to emphasize not only physical fitness and athletic competition, but also the "fun" aspects of sports, such as traditional play, community play, children's games, and social recreation.

Some schools have made basic fundamental development their major emphasis. In addition, enrichment programs for talented students in PE have become popular. These programs identify and encourage children to enhance their skills and interests. This might be a camping weekend (wall climbing, canoeing, fishing) or attendance at a college athletic contest. These directions will continue to challenge and tax the energies and talents of physical education specialists.

College courses offer similar opportunities for students at the postsecondary level. They also help prepare future teachers to teach such courses themselves. For instance, physical education activity courses offered by the University of Texas at Austin include:

Swimming	Racquetball
Judo/self-defense	Basketball
Scuba diving	Handball
Conditioning	Power volleyball
Dance	Fencing
Archery	Softball
Tennis	Karate/tae kwon do
Golf	

Duties and Activities of Teachers

Obviously, many demands and duties characterize the activities of the PE teacher. The physical education specialist as a teacher engages in some of the following activities:

1. Determines the ability of students in their courses.
2. Revises instruction based upon students' abilities; that is, when teaching a skill (such as throwing a ball) the PE instructor will structure the lesson relative to what the class is able to do and will proceed from that point.
3. Prepares the budget for equipment and materials and maintains them once obtained.
4. Utilizes an efficient system for reporting accidents and following up on them.
5. Conducts special programs for children with physiological and psychological problems.

6. Provides information to the parents and community concerning the curriculum.
7. Promotes physical fitness in the school and community.
8. Helps students to commit themselves to self-improvement.
9. Prompts nonparticipating learners to join class activities and stay involved.
10. Develops a wide variety of skills in students, such as accuracy, agility, balance, coordination, endurance, flexibility, power, rhythm, strength, timing, and other psychomotor abilities.

A Typical Day

The physical education instructor must maintain fitness not only as a model for students but to maintain the rigorous schedule that makes many demands upon him or her. Consider a single day in the life of a community college PE instructor who also serves as a basketball coach:

5:45 A.M.   Alarm clock rings.

6:30   Depart for college.

6:45   Arrive at gym and office.

6:50   Check dressing room to see if everything is in order for the game—warm-ups, uniforms, shoes, socks, and training supplies.

7:00   Make a short tape over the phone for radio broadcast. Leave any game-related information for the athletic office secretary.

7:45   Review for class.

8:00 to 8:45   Teach tennis class.

8:45 Talk with and help students after class.

9:15 Check to make sure the following are prepared for the game: officials, clock operator, thirty-second clock operator, ticket sellers, ticket takers, scorekeeper, announcer, concessions, and business office. Also call to make arrangements to have game videotaped.

10:00 Check mail. Check E-mail. Call opponent to check if everything is okay and obtain arrival time of team.

11:00 to 11:50 Swimming class.

Noon to 1:00 P.M. Lunch.

1:00 to 3:00 Office work.

3:00 to 3:30 Check out sound system, videotaping equipment, thirty-second and game clock, and all support personnel; have athletic secretary and cheerleaders call news media.

3:30 to 4:30 Go home, shower, and change for game.

4:35 Return to gym.

4:40 Double-check dressing rooms and gym lights. Go over game strategy.

5:30 Meet with team; discuss game plan.

6:00 Greet visiting team; manager shows them to locker room. Talk with opposing coach to see if everything is okay; may need location of a restaurant for postgame meal.

6:30 Taping and individual talks with players. Stretching exercises in locker room.

7:00 Team takes floor for warm-ups. Coaches report starting lineup.

7:15 Return to dressing room.

7:25 Return to court; coordinate player introductions.

7:30   Game begins.

9:00   Game concludes. Talk with team in the dressing room and then with the news media.

9:30   Check on dressing rooms; have managers and cheerleaders call news media not present at the game.

9:35   Prepare statistics.

10:30   Stop on the way home for a snack.

11:15   Prepare for following day's classes; prepare practice schedules.

12:00   Go to bed.

For those individuals who mesh teaching and coaching, it can be a truly demanding commitment. This combination requires intelligence, great energy, and ability. It also promises great rewards.

Educational Preparation for Teachers

Physical educators must obtain state certification as teachers. This takes place at a college that has an approved program for the education of PE teachers.

For example, prospective physical education teachers studying at Southern Utah University take a selection of the following courses (some of which are required and some of which may be chosen from several options), in addition to the general college requirements and electives:

Fundamentals of Individual and Dual Sports
Fundamentals of Team Sports
Health and Fitness Dynamics
Motor Learning
Kinesiology

Exercise Physiology
Athletic Training/Sports Medicine
Adaptive Physical Education
Teaching Individual, Dual, and Team Sports
Administration of Intramural/Physical Education/
  Athletics
Evaluation in Physical Education
Coaching Dance Teams and Drill Teams
Football Officiating
Baseball Officiating
Volleyball Officiating
Lifeguard Training
Water Safety Instructor Training
Physical Education Practicum
Psychosocial Aspects in Athletics
Methods of Teaching Elementary Physical Education
Methods of Teaching Secondary Physical Education
Student Teaching
Advanced First Aid–Emergency Care
Intermediate Swimming
Social Square Dance Fundamentals and Methods

In all programs for certification, in addition to professional physical education subjects, courses must be undertaken in the arts and sciences. Typically, these courses fall in areas such as communication skills, humanities, the natural sciences, mathematics, history, and social sciences.

A special experience characterizes the certification program of student teaching. This activity finds the college students, under the supervision of a cooperating teacher and a college faculty member, instructing school students. During this period of intensive training, the future teacher practices and refines the skills necessary for a practicing professional. In sports medicine it would be called an internship or residency.

Many physical educators pursue graduate courses and master's degrees; a few will earn doctorates; some will obtain graduate degrees in physical education; others will undertake work in other areas. Florida State University, as just one example, offers several graduate programs covering fitness-related areas such as teacher education, administration, athletics, and sports. Programs of study in the department of physical education include those leading to the master of science in physical education (with tracks in sport administration and teacher education in physical education); and the doctor of philosophy and doctor of education degrees in physical education with majors in sport administration and teacher education in physical education.

To teach at the college level, teacher certification or completion of teacher education courses is not required. Instead, the focus is on academic preparation at the college level. In most cases, an earned master's degree or doctorate is required to teach at the postsecondary level. However, situations differ, and usually community colleges require a master's and four-year institutions require a doctorate.

According to the U.S. Department of Labor, the majority of college professors earn between $33,000 and $85,000 yearly. Some experienced faculty members earn significantly more, especially in large universities.

Getting Started in Teaching

If physical education instruction may become your career, visit with a PE teacher and discuss your plans. He or she will be able to suggest colleges. In college, build into your educational program some courses in communication arts and business to permit greater flexibility upon graduation. Although teaching may be your first choice, career opportunities expand daily in sports and athletics and also exist as viable options. It is strongly suggested you obtain a student membership in your professional curriculum organization to help you stay current with your career and with potential job options.

For more information contact:

American Alliance for Physical Education, Health,
   Recreation and Dance
1900 Association Dr.
Reston, VA 20191
aahperd.org

Teaching Fitness Classes

Thanks to a growing interest in personal fitness, exercise classes and activities have become popular among virtually all age groups. From aerobics classes to those in more specialized areas of physical fitness, a demand has developed for trained fitness instructors. Many such roles do not normally require the years of formal education required of physical education teachers, and as such they can provide opportunities for almost any interested person to become involved at some level. Most typically, though, today's fitness instructor is a disciplined athlete who can set an excellent example for clients.

Serving as an instructor involves more than just an interest in people and health. Health fitness specialists need some training in physical education or exercise physiology. Good health and stamina, a pleasant personality, and the desire to help others are also necessary qualities for a health fitness career. Aspirants should have an interest in working with people of all ages, backgrounds, and abilities. They should possess the gift of inspiring confidence in others. Additional qualifications include emotional stability and maturity, a keen sense of humor, patience, ingenuity, and the ability to express oneself clearly both orally and in writing.

To use the industry vernacular, an instructor is one who works usually with a group in a more-or-less structured environment. Someone who teaches an aerobics class is thus an aerobics instructor. A trainer tends to work on a one-on-one basis with clients, often as a freelancer, and is generally associated with weight training or gymnastics, where a clear-cut goal is sought. A coach is someone who prepares a team or a professional athlete to meet a specific objective, such as placing in the Olympics.

The fitness instructor's place of employment varies. You might work in a large or small corporate or industrial firm's fitness center, a nursing home, preschool, hospital, dance studio, private club, community fitness center, or even on a cruise ship. There are a few areas in the industry in which you do not have to be a participant or maintain contact activity with clients. For example, you can be a wellness promoter by designing and/or managing programs, utilizing skills attained in business administration classes.

You should ask yourself several questions before embarking upon a career in health fitness. The aspiring trainer and instructor should consider the following:

1. Do I have the self-confidence and leadership skills to motivate others?

2. Am I comfortable working with a variety of client types and ages?

3. Do I assume responsibility for professional self-evaluation?
4. Do I understand how to create a safe class?
5. Do I have an understanding of anatomy, physiology, and nutrition?
6. Am I certified in CPR (cardiopulmonary resuscitation)?
7. Do I have an adequate educational background to screen clients for health problems?
8. Am I adequately trained in my area?
9. Am I physically fit role model for students?

Group-Exercise or Aerobics Instructors

Group exercise is a term that encompasses all forms of exercise set to music. Group-exercise instructors lead group classes or give individual instruction. They demonstrate an exercise, explain its purpose, supervise clients to ensure that the exercise is being done correctly, set the pace, and determine the number and sequence of exercises. In many situations they also set the length of the class or program. The group-exercise instructor can choose to work full-time, part-time, or casually, as needed. Formats vary from beginning to advanced aerobics, Jazzercise, aquacize, stretch-and-tone, and prenatal/postpartum.

Another exciting area within this field is that of the travel instructor. Travel instructors teach vacationers on cruise ships. Others may fly to various cities or countries as a representative of their fitness organizations. Some may work at the fitness center of a luxury hotel or a summer health resort. Participants may be toddlers, teenagers, pre- or postnatal women, fifty-plus, overweight individuals, athletes, or dance instructors themselves. It is the instructor's responsibility to seek any additional educational preparation necessary to teach individuals who need special attention. Lacking the knowledge required to deal effectively with these various groups can lead to unnecessary injury to clients and possible lawsuits for the instructor. It is, therefore, foolish for any instructor to accept a position for which he or she is not fully prepared.

No matter which path of group exercise you take, you will need adequate training with a basic course in anatomy/physiology and CPR. You will need the knowledge of health appraisal techniques, risk factor identification, and submaximal exercise testing results to properly recommend an exercise program. In addition, you should be able to demonstrate appropriate techniques in motivation, counseling, teaching, and behavior modification to promote lifestyle changes. If you plan to become an independent contractor, you should also have experience teaching and choreographing group exercise.

If you teach in a small organization such as an independent health club, community center, or private company, you will teach classes with music and routines that either you or the organization have designed. It may be your responsibility to update music or routines at designated intervals, or this may be a joint decision to be made with other instructors. In large franchise organizations, the organization will probably provide the music and choreography on a routine basis. You may also be required to do studio maintenance or act as a salesperson or receptionist. Make sure you find out if any other duties are included in your job description.

Your position in an organization determines certain obligations. If you are considered an employee, you may need to do more than just instruct your class. You may also need to sweep the floors and/or perform other needed functions. If you own your own business, you will probably be able to have someone else sweep the floors so that you will be able to concentrate on teaching exercise classes. Owning your own business is covered in Chapter 10.

As an independent contractor, you are self-employed and can teach as many classes as you desire, keeping in mind that you yourself should not overexercise. You should be providing your students a safe role model to follow. Your places of employment are unlimited. You may choose, for example, to teach exercise to employees of a large insurance firm in the company gym. Schools, nursing homes, dance studios, and houses of worship are all potential places of employment for the independent contractor.

Fitness centers are no longer found only in urban centers and country resorts. Many cruise lines hire exercise instructors to provide their passengers with the opportunity for a good workout. Travel instructors teach various classes each day to all ages and types of people. Your clients may be on a business trip or just seeking pleasure and relaxation. This is a highly competitive area. If you enjoy adventure, your fringe benefits may include working at exclusive spas or on cruise ships. You may even be selected to travel to other countries to teach. Therefore, to be favorably considered, you need to apply for this type of position, preferably after you have successfully taught group-exercise classes for some time.

The cost of getting started varies. Often, in smaller organizations it costs nothing to get started, although you may be required to purchase a uniform and pay for your training or certification. Training and certification costs vary greatly. If you wish to become connected with a large organization, you may have to pay franchise fee costs such as uniforms, music, and training.

Traveling instructors usually provide their own music because of the variety of classes they teach. The organization that hires you may expect you to buy your own exercise clothing and shoes.

A group-exercise instructor working in a small organization may make an hourly wage of $20 to $60. Employees of large organizations can make a slightly higher hourly wage. In a franchise position, the average income could be more than $25,000 to $30,000 per year for a part-time commitment, although keep in mind that income in this area varies widely.

For additional information contact:

International Fitness Association
12472 Lake Underhill Rd.
Orlando, FL 32828
ifafitness.com

International Fitness Professionals Association
14509 University Point Pl.
Tampa, FL 33613
ifpa-fitness.com

Canadian Association of Fitness Professionals
2851 John St.
P.O. Box 42011
Markham, ON
Canada L3R 5R7
canfitpro.com

Corporate Fitness Instructors

The concept of fitness has changed in recent years, and so has corporate America. Across the nation, corporate fitness programs have been developed to help employees keep healthy, active, and productive. Many companies now offer some form of fitness program for their employees. Corporate programs may focus not only on physical fitness but on mental fitness as well and include programs that help employees expand into a positive fitness lifestyle. In many corporate programs, cardiovascular fitness classes, such as aerobics, walking, jogging, swimming, and cross-country skiing, are popular offerings. From the corporate perspective, these classes help reduce the incidence of cardiovascular disease and its astronomical costs to the company. The incidence of chronic back pain and repetitive stress injury are also diminished, as morale and team spirit is increased.

A corporate fitness instructor may work in a large or small business, government organization, or hospital providing individual and/or group programs for employees, based on specific needs. You may find that if you are hired in this position, you might work either in a company's meeting room or fitness center or teach the company's employees at a local gym. The instructor may work with the company's medical staff in preparing programs. Employees are provided with a comprehensive fitness and lifestyle assessment, education in lifestyle change, and exercise classes. In some situations, because the program is designed to meet the employee's needs, you will be involved in program planning as well.

Some firms provide their employees with training in motivation boosting, leadership, and CPR, which helps the company improve productivity. If the company uses employee volunteers, they become actively involved in program planning and may lead fitness classes. Employees may pay yearly dues to support their fitness program. Participants get consistent reinforcement and the information necessary to make changes in lifestyle habits.

Many companies offer complete wellness programs such as stress reduction, smoking cessation, fitness testing, and nutritional evaluation, in addition to group exercise. Larger firms may have their own weight and exercise rooms. Taking this comprehensive approach to fitness not only enhances the employee's motivation to exercise, but allows the fitness instructor to screen employees for potential health risks.

Employers often look for people with an exercise physiology background coupled with knowledge of fitness testing, nutrition, stress management, business management, and human relations. Job candidates also should be prepared to teach workshops on stretching as a preventive measure for back pain and repetitive stress injury. A fitness pro should be adept at communicating with others and dealing with the variety of reactions he or she is likely to encounter among the participants in the programs.

In the corporate setting, a bachelor's degree in exercise physiology, physical education, or a related field along with professional certification is the minimum requirement. It is preferable that job candidates hold either a master's degree or be matriculated in a graduate program. Larger firms that offer tuition reimbursement programs to their employees may extend this benefit to the fitness director as well.

For additional information contact:

Association for Worksite Health Promotion
60 Revere Dr., Ste. 500
Northbrook, IL 60062
ahp7.org
(formerly the Association for Fitness in Business)

Group and Personal Trainers

As a personal trainer you may spend your winters on the French Riviera. Or, you might be the trainer for a Hollywood movie star. One-on-one instruction, though, requires more expertise than teaching an aerobics class. Even if you are qualified, you may find that personal training is not suited to your personality. One-on-one training takes more energy than teaching a class. You have to understand the strengths and weaknesses of your clients. You also have to be more personally involved. A personal trainer spends several hours with each client doing a fitness assessment and taking a personal history. You would also take a medical history and request a doctor's consent, if necessary. In addition, you should know about your client's daily diet, habits, and goals. You should check her or him for flexibility, strength, and stamina. You should ask the client, "What do you want to attain? Do you want to do aerobics? Do you want to stretch and tone? Do you want to build muscle? Do you want to lose your gut?" Make sure you know what your client wants. You may have to work around the schedule of a busy executive or celebrity. Your client may have physical limitations or injuries or need personalized prescriptions or monitoring. People who travel may want a personal trainer to come to their hotel to work with them. There are others who take their personal trainers with them to travel around the world so that they can keep up their exercise routines. Most personal trainers average three clients a day. Most trainers agree that you should start by working with one or two people you know to get a feel for the work and see whether you really like it.

Education, training, and background of trainers vary widely. Some have formal education in physical education, while others have a master's degree in exercise physiology. There are trainers who have a background in dance and others in weight training. A medical background, such as nursing, is also a valuable tool for the personal trainer to have. The main focus of personal trainers should be to continue to take courses and attend seminars to update their knowledge in health fitness.

Personal trainers also should prepare for certification from one or more of the internationally recognized sports and fitness organizations. A poorly prepared trainer can cause more harm than good, and there is also the issue of liability, so anyone who makes his or her primary income from training should research professional liability possibilities.

You can obtain more information from:

American Association of Personal Trainers
P.O. Box 11177
Newport Beach, CA 92658
aapt.net

American Council on Exercise
4851 Paramount Dr.
San Diego, CA 92123
acefitness.org

Yoga Instructors

Relaxation is as important to good health as exercise because it relieves tension. Yoga is an exercise system, formulated in the ashrams (places where people meet for spiritual instruction) of India centuries ago, that takes the entire human being into account more naturally than almost any other training system. Because the mind, body, and spirit interconnect, yoga teaches how to sustain yourself in peace and comfort throughout life. Yoga is a form of disciplined practice that promotes mental and physical well-being through physical postures called *asanas*, which are performed in correlation with proper breathing technique. Studies have shown that the relaxation posture effectively reduces high blood pressure.

Many physicians now recommend yoga to combat back ailments, sleeping disorders, and other stress-related problems. It is an excellent technique to aid an individual's mental well-being.

Integrating yoga postures and principles into one's schedule can add dimensions of flexibility, stamina, breathing control, relaxation, and mental astuteness that will inject new life into your aerobics and strength workouts. Instructors are employed by small and large organizations, including schools, health clubs, churches, and private homes.

A yoga instructor has usually studied and trained under the direction of a master yoga instructor. Instructors are responsible for leading a class through asanas and, in some situations, meditation as well. Although the postures look simple, they can be quite difficult for a beginner. It can take about ten weeks to teach a person how to relax quickly and deeply. Instructors assess individual students for proper body alignment and breathing technique. Some instructors also teach nutrition classes, and others work with special-needs groups such as the disabled, elderly, and HIV-positive. Yoga instructors may have been educated through courses in an academic setting, attending seminars, or self-study.

Qualifications should include emotional stability, patience, and a calm, warm personality. Yoga instructors should possess the ability to "choreograph" their asanas in a smooth, flowing manner so that the client is completely relaxed at the end of the session. An instructor should be able to choose music that is soothing and calming for the participants.

Study and practice under the direction of a yoga instructor is usually all that is required to qualify you to teach yoga, but it is advisable to check on teaching certification in any given locality. Although it is not mandatory, a teaching certificate indicates that serious time and interest have been invested in the subject. To gain a further edge in the market, aspiring yoga instructors should consider attending workshops in reflexology, nutrition, and exercise physiology.

For more information contact:

American Yoga Association
P.O. Box 19986
Sarasota, FL 34276
americanyogaassociation.org

8

Sports Medicine and
Related Careers

Perhaps the fastest-growing careers associated with sports have been those in sports medicine. The explosion of injuries at all levels and a desire by players, parents, and coaches to reduce them has created a greatly expanded need for sports medicine personnel. A growing concern with legal liability has also contributed to this movement. At the professional level, team owners, who pay players outstanding salaries, have hired people, purchased equipment, and established training programs to keep them healthy.

Historically, sports medicine personnel would attend to athletes only after they had been injured. Now strong emphasis has been placed upon injury avoidance, which can be accomplished largely through conditioning. The new emphasis can be seen from the following Athlete's Bill of Rights:

Proper Conditioning
Proper conditioning helps to prevent injuries by hardening the body and increasing resistance to fatigue.

1. Are prospective players given directions and activities for preseason conditioning?
2. Is there a minimum of two weeks of practice before the first game or contest?
3. Is each player required to warm up thoroughly prior to participation?
4. Are substitutions made without hesitation when players show evidence of disability?

Careful Coaching

Careful coaching leads to skillful performance, which lowers the incidence of injuries.

1. Is emphasis given to safety in teaching techniques and elements of play?
2. Are injuries carefully analyzed to determine causes and suggest preventive programs?
3. Are tactics discouraged that may increase the hazards and thus the incidence of injuries?
4. Are practice periods carefully planned and of reasonable duration?

Good Officiating

Good officiating promotes enjoyment of the game as well as the protection of players.

1. Are players as well as coaches thoroughly schooled in the rules of the games?
2. Are rules and regulations strictly enforced in practice periods as well as in games?

3. Are officials employed who are qualified both emotionally and technically for their responsibilities?

Equipment and Facilities

The right equipment and facilities serve a unique purpose in the protection of players.

1. Is the best protective equipment provided for contact sports?
2. Is careful attention given to proper fitting and adjustment of equipment?
3. Is equipment properly maintained, and are worn and outmoded items discarded?
4. Are proper areas for play provided and carefully maintained?

Medical Care

Adequate medical care is a necessity in the prevention and control of athletic injuries.

1. Is there a thorough preseason health history and medical examination?
2. Is a physician present at contests and readily available during practice sessions?
3. Does the physician make the decision as to whether an athlete should return to play following injury during games?
4. Is authority from a physician required before an athlete can return to practice after being out of play because of disabling injury?
5. Is the care given athletes by coach or trainer limited to first aid and medically prescribed services?

The importance of proper conditioning involving strength, cardiovascular fitness, and flexibility cannot be overemphasized. Listed below are the Ten Cardinal Principles of Athletic Conditioning that every coach, player, and sports medicine professional must know and implement.

1. **Warm-up.** Each activity must be preceded by an adequate warm-up. Following this step, stretching activities and running will provide the greatest benefit. Warming down likewise requires attention.
2. **Gradual starts.** Start slowly to condition someone and look to peak at a certain time. Setting goals can be helpful.
3. **Timing.** Athletes must be counseled not to overdo workouts; relaxation and rest are a part of every conditioning program.
4. **Intensity.** Quality and continuous activity with appropriate rest periods must characterize workouts and practices.
5. **Capacity level.** While cautious to avoid the above pitfalls, athletes will want to work to capacity and should have the encouragement to do so.
6. **Strength.** Greater endurance, speed, flexibility, and confidence will result from improved strength. This will also decrease vulnerability to injury.
7. **Motivation.** Sports medicine personnel can reinforce the coaches' techniques to stimulate players.
8. **Specialization.** Include in each player's conditioning program exercises that target his or her weaknesses in relation to the sport played.
9. **Relaxation.** Trainers should familiarize themselves with specific techniques to teach players how to relax and thereby recover from tension, fatigue, and stress.

10. **Routine**. A planned daily, weekly, and monthly routine must be constructed for each player in cooperation with the athlete and coach.

The above principles should serve as guidelines. Careful adherence can make an important difference to athletes. For example, in the area of warming up, one study at Duke University found that over 50 percent of injuries occur in the first quarter! In addition, the author has further observed that many injuries occur in the beginning of practice. Consequently, it's a must for players to warm up, even if they are late and practice has already begun.

An examination of the careers related to sports medicine follows.

Athletic Trainers

An athletic trainer's duties consist of the implementation of an injury prevention program and the initiation of immediate treatment and rehabilitation procedures for the injured athlete as directed by the team physician. He or she is the person you see down on the field or sitting on the bench close to the large first aid kit. Long before the contest, the trainer has prepared the participants, taping some and providing therapy for others. The trainer will stay after the game, providing services as needed.

Specifically, trainers engage in the following activities:

1. Design and monitoring of a program of conditioning in cooperation with the coaching staff.
2. Supervision of safety factors involving playing areas.
3. Selection of proper equipment in cooperation with the coaching staff and equipment manager.
4. Administration of first aid to injured athletes.

5. Application of devices such as braces and bandages to prevent injury.
6. Development and supervision of the rehabilitation program for an injured athlete under the supervision of a physician. This may involve the use of whirlpool or ultrasound equipment. Often the trainer will show the athlete exercises to do to prevent a recurring injury and then monitor the improvement of muscle strength.
7. Maintenance of the athletic training area and performance of tasks such as ordering supplies, supervising the servicing of equipment, and keeping careful records.
8. Development of good working relationships with the players, coaches, physicians, and with the school authorities or professional management.

Obviously the duties and obligations are quite significant and the athletic trainer's importance to sports continues to increase. The late Otho Davis, head trainer for the Philadelphia Eagles and executive director of the National Athletic Trainers Association, said that the most important role of the trainer is to prevent an injury from occurring, because at the professional level a player cannot afford to miss practice. For most professional athletes, conditioning occurs eleven months a year! After a month break following the end of the season for their respective sports, many players begin a new training program consisting of running, weight training, or other activities.

Another area of recent concern is that of injury prevention as related to equipment selection. The trainer works as a member of a team, which includes the coach and equipment manager, and is guided by the following in choosing equipment:

1. Its specifications must provide maximum protection for the area to be protected.
2. It must be able to withstand repeated use with no decrease in efficiency.
3. It must fit carefully so that it can provide protection under playing conditions.
4. It must not impede the player's activity (as nearly as possible).
5. It must not create a hazard to other contestants. States and leagues usually have a rule against this.
6. It must be replaced when it is no longer effective and has lost its protective value.

Athletic training offers a demanding and an enjoyable career for persons interested in athletics. The working conditions and salary vary greatly. At the school level, most teach courses and serve as trainers part-time, for which they receive additional compensation similar to coaches.

According to Indiana University, beginning athletic trainers can expect salaries of $23,000 per year; experienced trainers can earn more. In a recent survey conducted by the National Athletic Trainers Association, a majority of men reported a beginning salary between $25,000 and $40,000 yearly, and over 40 percent of women reported starting salaries of $20,000 to $35,000.

College trainers work full-time in this capacity and enjoy greater prestige than their high school counterparts, but they have similar salaries. Those who teach and serve as trainers at the university level earn considerably more. Professional trainers' salaries vary with the team; some work part-time only when the sport is in season, others work year-round and receive good salaries.

Once you believe you have the physical and psychological qualities to become an athletic trainer, begin by taking science-related courses in high school (health, chemistry, and so forth). Talk with your school counselor concerning your interest and obtain information about colleges with programs approved by the National Athletic Trainers Association. In college you will take both liberal arts (English, history, science) and professional education subjects.

For example, Colby-Sawyer College in New Hampshire offers the following athletic training courses:

Taping Techniques in Athletic Training
Prevention and Care of Athletic Injuries
Athletic Training Assessment
Athletic Training Practicum
Field Experience in Athletic Training
Therapeutic Modalities
Clinical Interventions in Health Psychology
Therapeutic Rehabilitation
Structural Kinesiology
Exercise Physiology
Biomechanics
Athletic Health Care Administration
Pathology of the Body Systems
Pharmacological Concepts in Health Care

In addition to completing the courses for graduation, a significant number of hours of practical work and an examination must be passed for NATA certification as an athletic trainer. Persons may obtain approval in other ways: the apprenticeship program (for persons graduating from colleges not offering athletic training);

graduation from a physical therapy program; and through special arrangements for trainers with experience.

Many opportunities for positions in athletic training will exist in the years ahead. For more information contact:

National Athletic Trainers Association
2952 Stemmons Freeway
Dallas, TX 75247-6916
nata.org

Sports Physicians

At the center of the sports medicine profession are the sports medicine physicians—orthopedists, osteopaths, and chiropractors. Regardless of the specialty of the physician, the commandments of Theodore Fox, M.D., formerly of the Chicago Bears professional football team, deserve serious attention as guidelines to behavior. These have undergone slight modification to conform to this book.

Sports Physician's Ten Commandments

1. The physician must be trained in all procedures for prevention, recognition, diagnosis, and treatment of injuries; first aid as well as knowledge of soft tissue and skeletal injuries.

2. The physician must personally examine and evaluate all candidates for the sport or team prior to their participation to determine each individual's fitness for the same. This should include a history on all previous illnesses, accidents, and surgical procedures as well as a psychological evalua-

tion and a thorough physical examination. The physical
evaluation should include observations of any physical
characteristics and defects predisposing the player to injury,
especially in the collision sports. The physical examination
should include determination of the individual's maturity,
balance, coordination, agility, stamina, and strength.

3. The physician must know the basic fundamentals of the
   particular sport with which he or she is involved to better
   understand the mechanism of the injuries occurring, as
   well as the injured participant and her or his problem.

4. The physician must observe and evaluate the emotional
   well-being of the athlete, especially the young player. Is the
   candidate being pushed by a frustrated parent to be a
   superstar or made apprehensive by a parent because he or
   she might get hurt?

5. The physician should fit and select all protective gear and
   equipment and check it as to type and quality, especially in
   the collision sports.

6. The physician should supervise the trainer or the coach in
   the proper use of physiotherapeutic techniques used in the
   training room. Also, the physician is responsible for conditioning and rehabilitation exercises (such as weight training). Upon the doctor rests the responsibility for total
   rehabilitation of the injured athlete (mental and physical);
   a careful examination must precede returning to
   participation.

7. The physician must advise the coach not to teach danger-
   ous blocking and checking practices and about the avoidance of mismatches between athletes, especially young
   players. The doctor should advise the coach or trainer

about problems or injuries that may occur because of heat, humidity, overwork, or fatigue.

8. The physician (or a designated replacement) must be available at all times to examine the injured player as soon as possible after the injury. This is especially true in collision sports where, if possible, the physician should be on the field. Often youngsters will mask an injury so as to continue to play; a physician can make an assessment of the severity of the injury. Also, certain injuries (neck, re-injury) require a doctor's examination.

9. The physician must prevent an injured player from returning to the game if there is a reasonable doubt about the player's condition. In doing so the physician must resist all pressures from coaches, parents, alumni, and the player.

10. The doctor must obtain x-rays of injuries (and other information as necessary) prior to judging the condition of the injury.

Those considering a career as a sports physician should realize the academic commitment necessary. Excellent grades and an interest and competence in science are a must.

If you're planning a career in this area, a long commitment to academics is necessary. In addition, these specialties require passing a licensure examination to practice medicine in the state of your choice.

Sports physicians have a strong interest in improving their profession, and many conduct research on various aspects of athletic performance. In addition, these individuals work well with people and have a strong interest in athletics and sports.

For more information contact:

American Medical Association
535 N. State St.
Chicago, IL 60610
ama-assn.org

Orthopedists

Although some teams employ general practitioners (GPs) in the capacity of sports physicians, orthopedists by their training best serve in this position. Orthopedists are medical doctors (M.D.s) who treat injuries to the skeletal system—backs, necks, arms, legs and joints, and to the body's muscles. Those involved in sports normally serve on a consulting basis with teams and/or work in sports clinics.

They are the geniuses and miracle doctors who frequently save careers, improve the quality of lives, and lead in developing new surgical procedures. Consequently, this career is the best paid of all sports medicine personnel. Yearly salaries of more than $250,000 are common. In addition, they enjoy fine working conditions and, in most cases, great prestige. These doctors attend undergraduate college and then enter medical school. After graduation they concentrate on their chosen field. This involves more course work, individual study, and a practical experience. The internship takes one year and the residency normally four years, so the total education of the orthopedist takes nine years after college! During the residency period, the young doctor works under the supervision of an experienced orthopedic physician, conducting examinations, directing first aid, performing surgery, and designing rehabilitation programs. Not all orthopedists go into sports medicine; some set up private practice and work to correct deformities related mainly to muscle, joint, and bone problems. If a person has a serious accident requiring surgery, such as cartilage damage to a knee or a hip replacement, an orthopedist would be involved. With increased attention to injury prevention and rehabilitation, opportunities for careers as a doctor with a specialty in orthopedics will continue to be very good.

For more information contact:

Association of American Medical Colleges
2450 N St. NW
Washington, DC 20037
aamc.org

Osteopaths

Osteopathic physicians (D.O.s) concentrate on the musculoskeletal system of the body in returning the injured athlete to action. Like medical doctors, they utilize surgery, drugs, and other acceptable health care practices. In addition, they may use manipulation and emphasize the treatment of the whole athlete in designing a conditioning or rehabilitation program.

Although still not totally accepted by medical doctors, osteopathic medicine has made great gains in recent years, and some professional sports teams utilize D.O.s as their team physicians. The educational requirements of osteopathic college almost parallel those of medical colleges, and D.O.s wishing to specialize likewise complete a rigorous residency.

Salaries of doctors of osteopathy tend to lag behind those of medical doctors. However, most do well (often earning more than $100,000 a year), and those in sports medicine may do even better. Opportunities for employment for osteopaths in the future will continue to remain very good as sports medicine expands and the public comes to further respect the work of doctors of osteopathic medicine.

For more information contact:

American Osteopathic Association
142 E. Ontario St.
Chicago, IL 60611
aoa-net.org

Chiropractors

Doctors of chiropractic emphasize the utilization of manipulation (adjustments) as their primary treatment. They do not believe in using prescription drugs or surgery, nor are they permitted to do so by state law (although they often work as part of a team with M.D.s who may prescribe appropriate drugs). Chiropractors do employ other treatments with the injured athlete—heat, water, diet, nutritional supplementation, massage therapy, and others.

Chiropractic colleges require two years of college as a condition of enrollment. At these colleges, students pursue courses in the biological sciences and in chiropractic principles and also undertake a clinical experience. Most chiropractors earn somewhere between $44,000 and $106,000 annually, with an average of about $82,000, according to the U.S. Department of Labor. The growing interest in holistic medicine and the unique contribution of chiropractic to sports medicine will ensure growing opportunities for interested individuals.

For more information contact:

American Chiropractic Association
1701 Clarendon Blvd.
Arlington, VA 22209
amerchiro.org

Physical Therapists

The field of sports physical therapy has advanced tremendously over the past couple of decades. Physical therapists who specialize in sports-related maladies serve not only school, college, and professional athletes along with weekend athletes, but also others who wish to avail themselves of the aggressive innovative techniques of sports physical therapy to return to maximum health as soon as possible.

Physical therapists work with athletes who have been disabled through accident, birth defect, or illness. Some therapists work with athletes sent to them by a physician, to aid in the rehabilitation of an injury. Treatments include exercises for increasing strength, endurance, coordination, and range of motion; activities to facilitate motor capacity or learning; instruction in activities of daily living and use of assistance devices; and application of physical agents such as heat and cold, sound, water, and acupuncture to relieve pain and/or alter physiological status.

Physical therapists attend college to receive certification in their profession; some attend graduate programs and enter leadership positions in the field. Certification requires pursuing certain course work and, in most states, passing an examination to receive a license to treat patients.

Many physical therapists who work with athletes do so at sports medicine clinics where they assist other professionals in rehabilitating athletes. This team approach typically involves working with many athletes and coaches rather than just a single team. According to the U.S. Department of Labor, the majority of physical therapists in all areas of employment earn between $46,000 and $68,000 yearly. Insiders believe salaries as well as overall opportunities will grow as the sports profession and the public continue to realize the value of physical therapy.

Physical Therapy Paraprofessionals

Two types of paraprofessionals also work in the area of physical therapy—the physical therapist assistant and the physical therapy aide. The former graduates from a two-year program with a major in physical therapy; the latter learns on the job. Both work under the supervision of a professional physical therapist, who in turn works under the supervision of a physician. Salaries for assistants range in the $29,000 to $41,000 category, with a median of about $34,000. Median earnings for aides are about $20,000. These job roles provide viable options for those not wanting to complete four years (or more) of college.

For more information about these specialties contact:

American Physical Therapy Association
1111 N. Fairfax St.
Alexandria, VA 22314
apta.org

A periodical with valuable information for those considering entering the physical therapy field is *Rehab Management*; it contains articles such as "Sports Injury Management" and "Taking a Proactive Approach to Sports Medicine Injuries." It may be purchased from:

CurAnt Communications
6701 Center Dr. West, Ste. 450
Los Angeles, CA 90045
rehabpub.com

Exercise Physiologists

Exercise physiology is the science that deals with the study of muscular activity and the associated functional responses and adaptations. Therefore, an exercise physiologist is interested in the influence of exercise on these body functions. An exercise physiologist must have a general understanding of the scientific bases underlying the exercise-induced physiological responses. He or she is an independent research scientist who has earned a doctoral degree with an emphasis in the life sciences and has a primary research interest in physical exercise.

Exercise physiologists conduct controlled investigations of responses and adaptations to muscular activity utilizing subjects in a clinical setting, a research institute, or an academic institution. In addition, they often teach academic courses in exercise physiology, environmental physiology, or applied human physiology for students of medicine, physiology, physical education, and other health-related fields. Some work at YMCAs, JCCs, and other community centers, or in commerce and industry, rehabilitation programs, and competitive sports programs.

If you are interested in working toward a Ph.D., which is necessary for research and/or college teaching, opportunities for graduate study are available within academic programs of medicine, physiology, biology, physical education, kinesiology, exercise science, and biochemistry at many universities.

To work in the commercial/industrial area, you would need a degree from the department of physical education, exercise science, or health science and nutrition. Any health-related setting that employs exercise physiologists will require a degree in health science, physical therapy, physical education, kinesiology, or exercise science.

The undergraduate curriculum is influenced by an individual's career choice. Preparation in general biology, chemistry, biochemistry, physics, mathematics, and computer science is important if a research and teaching career is desired. In some professional programs, the curriculum is well defined. For some employment opportunities, the undergraduate student can select valuable training in specific areas that are more directly applicable.

Students interested in exercise physiology should visit the various types of employment settings to gain further insight concerning the necessary training and background, the certification prerequisites, the job responsibility, the general work environment, and the employment potential.

Dance/Movement Therapists

The dance/movement therapist uses movement in the treatment and rehabilitation of children and adults with neurological or other physical impairments and/or social, emotional, or cognitive challenges. This work is distinguished from other types of dance by its focus on the nonverbal aspects of behavior and its use of movement. A dance/movement therapist, also referred to simply as a dance therapist, works with people who require special psychotherapeutic services because of behavioral, learning, perceptual, and/or physical disorders. The therapist uses knowledge of how the body moves in relation to space and rhythm, which helps a person develop coordination, improve gait, and correct problems in mobility. The emotionally impaired are assisted by the dance therapist's observations, which aid in the development of a behavior modification program utilizing dance and music.

Skilled dance/movement therapists must be well trained in the art of dance and well versed in psychopathology and human development. Dance/movement therapists are employed in psychiatric hospitals, clinics, day treatment programs, community mental health centers, developmental centers, correctional facilities, special schools, and rehabilitation facilities. They work with people of all ages and in all socioeconomic levels, in both group and individual situations. Job opportunities for trained professionals vary in different locations. Many dance/movement therapists are pioneering job development in their region, and the American Dance Therapy Association has, since its inception in 1966, striven to enhance job opportunities for dance/movement therapists.

A bachelor's or master's degree in special education, kinesiology, psychology, or a related field may be sufficient if the person's dance background is very strong and if he or she has additional dance therapy training and a supervised clinical internship. The American Dance Therapy Association recommends that students preparing for a career as a dance/movement therapist first obtain a broad liberal arts background with an emphasis in psychology, in addition to extensive training in a wide variety of dance forms. Students should also study choreography and kinesiology.

Professional training is concentrated at the master's level. Studies include courses such as dance/movement therapy theory and practice, human development, observation and research skills, and a supervised internship in a clinical setting. Candidates may apply for certification as a DTR (Dance Therapist Registered), which qualifies master's degree recipients to work in a professional treatment system. Candidates may also apply for the ADTR distinction (Academy of Dance Therapists Registered), which demonstrates additional requirements have been met qualifying the recipient to teach, provide supervision, and engage in private practice.

For more details contact:

American Dance Therapy Association
200 Century Plaza, Ste. 108
Columbia, MD 21044
adta.org

Occupational Therapists

Occupational therapists work with persons who have experienced physical injuries or illnesses, sensory or tactile deficiencies, psychological or developmental disorders, or problems and impediments associated with the aging process. The occupational therapist coordinates a variety of educational, vocational, and rehabilitation therapies to allow the patient to become as self-sufficient as possible and lead as normal a life as possible in work, education, and pleasure. Tact, creativity, ability to solve complex living problems, and an interest in helping others are necessary. Occupational therapists work in hospitals, clinics, extended care facilities, rehabilitation hospitals, government agencies, and community agencies.

Four years of college with a major in occupational therapy is the training required to become an occupational therapist. Most states require occupational therapists to obtain a license to practice. Applicants must have a degree or post-undergraduate certification from an accredited school before they can sit for the National Certification Examination, which is required to become a registered occupational therapist. A master's degree or a certificate program can be taken for those who already have an undergraduate degree in occupational therapy.

According to the American Occupational Therapy Association, full-time occupational therapists have median incomes of about $45,000, and some with advanced degrees earn more than $60,000 annually.

More details about this field are available from:

American Occupational Therapy Association
4720 Montgomery La.
P.O. Box 31220
Bethesda, MD 20824-1220
aota.org

Canadian Association of Occupational Therapists
CTTC Building, Ste. 3400
1125 Colonel By Dr.
Ottawa, ON
Canada K1S 5R1
caot.ca

Occupational Therapy Assistants

An occupational therapy assistant helps the occupational therapist conduct a series of educational, vocational, and rehabilitation activities aimed at enabling disabled individuals to reach their highest functional levels possible. An occupational therapy assistant works under the supervision of a registered occupational therapist and assists by preparing materials for activities, maintaining tools and equipment, and recording and reporting on a patient's progress. He or she may help teach patients to manipulate wheelchairs or to stretch and make limber certain muscles. Persons who seek employment as occupational therapy assistants should have a desire to help others and display understanding, tact, and patience when working with the disabled. Occupational therapy assistants work in hospitals, nursing homes, rehabilitation centers, psychiatric hospitals, and military and veterans hospitals.

Preparation for a career as an occupational therapy assistant can be achieved through a two-year associate degree program, through a one-year program at an accredited institution, or through a twenty-five-week program conducted in a hospital setting.

Earnings in this field average about $33,000 annually, according to the AOTA.

Occupational Therapy Aides

An occupational therapy aide assists the occupational therapist by preparing materials and equipment for use during patient treatment. An occupational therapy aide may also provide a range of clerical or other tasks such as scheduling appointments, restocking or ordering supplies, and filling out insurance forms. No formal education beyond a high school diploma is required, but applicants should possess strong interpersonal skills and a desire to help people in need.

Jobs for occupational therapy aides are often part-time positions.

Rehabilitation and Therapeutic Recreation Therapists

Rehabilitation therapists and therapeutic recreation therapists usually direct both indoor and outdoor activities. They may perform a great deal of physical exercise while conducting sports and dance programs. These specialists are employed in hospitals, rehabilitation centers, schools offering special education programs, nursing homes, correctional institutions, and homes for the aged.

Rehabilitation therapists are responsible for conducting, organizing, and administering recreation and leisure programs designed to aid in the recovery or improve the adjustment of persons who are ill, physically or mentally challenged, or behaviorally disturbed. They organize both individual and group activities for children as well as adults. Therapists often work with other professionals, including physicians, psychologists, psychiatrists, nurses, and teachers. They determine the needs of the individuals or groups and may recommend programs involving exercise, social participation, group interaction, or hobbies to meet the desired objectives. Therapists encourage individuals to participate in the selected activities and offer assistance, instruction, and leadership when necessary. They observe the individuals during the program and prepare reports to aid in evaluating their social, mental, or physical progress. Other members of the health care team will use these reports to coordinate patient care.

Therapists employed by rehabilitation institutions may consult with individuals who are being discharged, advising them of recreation programs and facilities in their communities and then arranging for their participation in these programs. Additional responsibilities of rehabilitation therapists may include hiring, training, and supervising both volunteer and paid recreation workers. They may also prepare and submit program budgets, order equipment and supplies, maintain accurate financial and personnel records, and analyze and make recommendations for improving the recreation program. In addition, they may be responsible for scheduling and supervising the use of all equipment and facilities.

Good physical health, stamina, a pleasant personality, and a sincere desire to help people are necessary for a career as a recreational therapist. You should have an interest in working with people of all ages and backgrounds and be able to inspire confidence in their capabilities. In addition, you should possess a keen sense of humor, patience, ingenuity, creative imagination, and the ability to express yourself clearly, be it orally, physically with the use of body language, or in writing. You will be a mentor and clinician for a wide gamut of people, from traumatized children to lonely and frightened seniors to accident survivors to patients devastated by AIDS.

Rehabilitation therapists should have an extensive knowledge of functional anatomy, exercise physiology, pathology, electrocardiography, human behavior/psychology, and gerontology as well as knowledge of the principles and practices of graded exercise testing, exercise prescription, exercise leadership skills, and emergency procedures. Courses in these disciplines are available at the undergraduate and graduate levels.

During high school, aspirants to this career should complete a college entrance program. It is important to include courses in public speaking, art, and music. Participation in as many sport and athletic activities as possible also is recommended.

Although an associate degree in recreational therapy from an accredited junior college or community college will qualify aspirants for jobs requiring far less specialized skills, completion of at least a bachelor's degree in recreation with an emphasis in rehabilitation or therapeutic recreation is recommended. Certification also should be sought as early as possible. Beginning with an associate degree may be a good route toward getting a job temporarily, while you continue schooling on a part-time basis. It can also serve the purpose of providing experience with work in the field to allow you to test your interest and commitment in this area. For more information contact:

American Therapeutic Recreation Association
1414 Prince St., Ste. 204
Alexandria, VA 22314
atra-tr.org

National Council for Therapeutic Recreation Certification
7 Elmwood Dr.
New City, NY 10956
nctrc.org

Kinesiology

Kinesiology, a diverse field having to do with body mechanics, offers a multitude of possibilities. Some physical therapists specialize in this branch of therapy. Graduates with degrees in kinesiology also can work as consultants to industries that make sporting equipment and attire, especially running shoes. Others go on to become rehabilitation or physical therapists themselves. Still others earn Ph.D.s and do research and teach in the field.

Nurses, nutritionists, nurse-midwives, hand therapists, and orthotists and prosthetists, among others, are all people who work in this rich and diverse field. Professionals in these areas work directly with patients in hospital settings, at home, and at play. Nurse-midwives, for example, require special training since they must undertake invasive procedures. Hand therapists are physical or occupational therapists who work exclusively with patients suffering impairments due to birth defects, accident or injury, age, arthritis, or repetitive strain syndrome owing to misuse of equipment at home or at the workplace. Certified orthotists (COs) and certified prosthetists (CPs) make and fit artificial limbs or devices to enable better use of damaged limbs.

Complementary Health Trainers

A strong movement exists in the country toward supporting conventional medicine with complementary strategies such as acupuncture, sports massage, and nutrition (diet, vitamin, mineral, herbal supplementation). In addition, some believe these procedures can have a beneficial effect on an athlete's performance.

Relatively few schools offer programs in the area of acupuncture; programs and courses in massage therapy are much more common (check the yellow pages or conduct a Web search for schools near you). In the latter area, students can take course work in the massage technician curriculum, obtain certification, and then move ahead to massage therapy. Studying acupuncture includes study of that technique but may also include herbology, therapeutic exercise, massage, and Asian physical therapy.

Sports massage continues to gain adherents, as does the acupuncture technique. The procedure focuses upon the nature of the athletic activity (for example, tennis players are treated differently than soccer players). Some massage therapists operate a private practice, others work at sports medicine clinics, and many obtain employment at health clubs. For additional information contact:

American Association of Acupuncture and Oriental Medicine
5530 Wisconsin Ave., Ste. 1210
Chevy Chase, MD 20815
aaom.org

American Massage Therapy Association
820 Davis St.
Evanston, IL 60201
amtamassage.org

Athletes long in the forefront of the nutrition movement have sought to "eat and win" and to supplement their diets with vitamins, minerals, and herbs to "gain an edge" over their opponents. Recently the positive research results on optimizing performance with supplementation combined with a strong desire to avoid drugs has enhanced this field among those in athletics.

Professional sports nutritionists may have backgrounds in medicine—physicians, nurses, and others who have obtained additional course work and certification; others, such as athletic coaches, physical therapists, and so forth, have attended special programs to study nutrition. The latter, while not entitled to be called nutritionists, do assist those in sports with diet suggestions. Some in this field have attended schools emphasizing holistic health and have an array of unproved but promising suggestions for athletes.

Those involved in this field work with sports medicine centers or in private practice providing advice to coaches and players. They have strong backgrounds in science (biochemistry in particular) and excellent interpersonal skills. In addition, most have a strong dedication to wellness for themselves and their clients. For additional information contact:

National Association of Sports Nutrition
7710 Balboa Ave., Ste. 227B
San Diego, CA 92111
nasnutrition.com

Other Sports Medicine Opportunities

The fabulous growth of sports medicine has touched every area of the medical and allied medical professions. Dentists, podiatrists, orthotists, prosthetists, optometrists, ophthalmologists, nutritionists, psychologists, and other specialists have applied their unique skills and knowledge to improve athletic performance. For example, dentists may work on special mouthpieces designed to improve strength and reduce fatigue for some athletes. Podiatrists prepare special inserts for shoes for injured athletes or those with chronic problems. Orthotists and prosthetists assist injured athletes with special equipment to return them to action and prevent re-injury. Optometrists and ophthalmologists, who are vision specialists, properly evaluate and fit athletes with corrective glasses. Some have had excellent success with vision exercises for improving athletic performance. The explosion of research linking diet and supplementation (using vitamins and minerals) and sports success has placed nutritionists in the forefront of the movement to reduce injuries and increase athletic performance. Psychologists help athletes improve performance through mental avenues.

Sports Medicine Clinics and Centers

In recent years, there has been an expanded interest in the team approach to the prevention and treatment of athletic injuries. The previous information on the athletic trainers, sports physicians, and physical therapists emphasized the importance of these individuals working together. In accordance with this team concept, there is a strong trend toward injured athletes being treated at sports medicine clinics or centers. Most often these exist in one of three settings: at universities related to medical schools, at hospitals, and at private enterprises in medical buildings. The former serves the college community, particularly the athletes as well as outsiders; frequently the center conducts research on new methods of conditioning and injury rehabilitation and often offers sports medicine clinics for coaches and others.

As sports medicine clinics and centers expand, they will be an important source of employment for athletic trainers, physical therapists, and physicians. They offer more flexibility in terms of activities than are traditionally found in these careers.

Sports medicine professionals make an important contribution to athletics. Sports enthusiasts with a bent toward science and health deserve to give these occupations serious consideration when choosing a career.

Getting Started

If you are a student, you can gain valuable experience while in high school or college by serving as a student athletic trainer. Such a person normally performs tasks such as the following:

1. Helps maintain the training room and the supplies.
2. Aids with the taping and treatments.
3. Prepares field kits and has them available during contests and practices.
4. Reports new injuries to coach and trainer.
5. Prepares beverages for athletes' breaks during games and practices.
6. Completes a course for student trainers.
7. Keeps student trainer duties separate from student manager responsibilities.
8. Aids in record keeping of player injuries and treatment.

9. Performs related tasks as asked by coach, trainer, or physician.
10. Maintains a positive working relationship with players, coaches, physicians, trainers, and with opposing teams and their personnel.

Many colleges and high schools utilize female student athletic trainers. Excellent career opportunities exist for female athletic trainers. Although women's entrance into the field initially was slow, it has continued to gain momentum. Regardless of gender, this field offers excellent potential for those with the right training and abilities.

In fact, opportunities throughout the broad area of sports medicine are promising. With the strong desire from all segments of society and the sports world to curtail athletic injuries, varied and profitable career opportunities can be anticipated in sports medicine for years to come.

Keep in mind that the more advanced areas of sports medicine require commitment, plain and simple. There are financial concerns, such as paying for professional education, and also time and logistical matters to consider. Becoming an osteopathic physician, for example, requires a four-year degree, four years of medical school, and one to three years of residency before becoming eligible to sit for a licensure exam. Medical students put in eighteen-hour days studying and making rounds, and the strain can be enormous. Chiropractic training is less rigorous and can be completed in six years. People considering these fields also need certain personal tools. They need maturity and dedication. They also need to achieve a substantial background in physiology, biochemistry, and biomechanics, as well as experience in working with people who may be physically restricted to varying degrees.

Rehabilitative therapists also need training in the sciences, particularly anatomy and biomechanics. For them, however, interpersonal skills are even more essential because they work intimately with patients and clients. Besides physical, occupational, and recreational therapists, there are assistant- and aide-level positions. These opportunities also require a deep commitment and additional training as the level of sophistication increases. The rewards, however, are great because rehabilitative therapists often see the results of their work and take great pride and pleasure in helping people.

9

FITNESS AND SPORTS BUSINESSES

ALTHOUGH PROFESSIONAL AND college sports, coaching, and other areas covered in previous chapters account for many career opportunities, they are not the only ones. In fact, the growing emphasis on exercise and physical fitness has created a variety of career possibilities for those interested in these areas.

Health Clubs and Fitness Centers

A health club or fitness center is a multifaceted fitness facility that, either by itself or as part of a larger chain operation, usually operates on a profit-making basis. The earliest health clubs were substantially different from today's fitness center, typically identifying themselves as health spas. Their focus was on relaxation features such as whirlpools, steam rooms, and body massage.

Today's facilities emphasize exercise rather than relaxation and provide a wealth of equipment, services, and fitness systems for their members to use. Many health clubs and fitness centers also provide clients with opportunities for swimming, running, stretching, and weight training. A full-service fitness center may feature aerobic conditioning equipment, exercise classes, and a spa area. Many also have tennis and racquetball courts.

Some of the careers discussed in this chapter are also open to those not working in a health club, but who are involved with other types of organizations.

Administrative Personnel

Administrative staff in health clubs and fitness centers includes managers, salespeople, and others who are concerned with the business side of the operation. An efficient staff can provide its members with a cost-effective, well-run facility. If the administration is weak, the club will probably have low standards and be disorganized, so examine the club carefully before you accept a job. Salaries in these areas are dependent upon club size and your education and experience.

Desk Receptionists

The desk receptionist is the first person that members and prospective members meet when they enter a facility. This person is the facility's public relations person, and the degree of friendliness and helpfulness you find here is representative of the facility as a whole. The receptionist's chief responsibility is to control the flow of traffic into the club and to answer the telephones. The receptionist also welcomes new members, provides them with basic information, and introduces them to a salesperson who will give them a tour and description of the programs available. The desk receptionist also may have responsibility for security, as the receptionist is the person who usually checks membership ID cards. This role may also involve E-mail communications and maintaining the organization's website.

Salespeople

The chief duty of salespeople is to sell club memberships. Salespeople tour the facility with prospective members and encourage membership. Salespeople may follow up with mailings and phone calls to those who do not immediately join. They often rely on commissions for their incomes, and weekly reports keep their employers informed about productivity.

Managers/Assistant Managers

A manager's responsibility is to coordinate the efforts of all administrative, fitness, and auxiliary personnel. The manager sets the tone for the entire club or center, and the quality of the facility is a reflection of the manager's concern and expertise. This is probably the most stressful position in a fitness organization, as the manager/assistant manager deals constantly with both the staff and the public.

Fitness Personnel

There are a number of positions that make up the ranks of fitness personnel.

Exercise Program Directors

The exercise program director heads the fitness staff. This key person must have a number of attributes in addition to a personal commitment to physical fitness. These skills include managing, testing, and communicating. The ability to plan, implement, and evaluate programs is critical. Exercise program directors design, implement, and administer safe, effective, and enjoyable preventive and rehabilitative exercise programs. They are responsible for seeing that class instructors and supervisors deliver a competent, consistent level of service. Therefore, they train their staffs, instilling the required knowledge, competencies, and skills necessary for administration of these tests and activities. The director educates and communicates with members of the community about exercise programs. A qualified director usually has a background oriented more toward exercise than business. The director may have a degree in physical education or exercise physiology, certification in sports medicine, or training in another related area.

Exercise Test Technologists

These are staff with training in how to test the following: standing height, weight, resting heart rate, resting blood pressure, and body composition. Technologists administer, under appropriate direction, graded exercise testing procedures consistent with the individual's age and health status and record data collected before, during, and after the graded exercise test. If necessary, they are able to implement emergency procedures and thus need current certification in cardiopulmonary resuscitation (CPR).

Consultants

The consultant may be an individual, such as a physician who specializes in sports medicine, or a firm that advises on physical testing and profiling. A good consultant is usually someone who does not represent specific manufacturers within the fitness industry;

instead, this individual has a broad interest and background in overall development of fitness programs.

Martial Arts Instructors

The martial arts encompass many forms of study and practice such as karate, tai chi, judo, aikido, and tae kwon do, to name a few. Each area has its own requirements in order to earn belts and/or degrees that would enable one to become an instructor. The teaching of self-defense has become a very popular addition to many clubs, and the training requirements for instructors are stringent, due largely to the potential for injury in these strenuous physical activities.

Each specialty in this group requires a specific progression of skill development to reach each level of recognition. If you are interested in the martial arts, you should discuss your training program with well-recognized instructors in your area and plan to work for several different organizations to see if you enjoy this type of employment.

Lifeguards

Lifeguards coordinate and control pool traffic, maintaining safety for all in the pool and its immediate environment. Lifeguards are also responsible for checking the temperature and quality of the pool's water several times a day. In many facilities, the lifeguard is also required to teach swimming classes, often to people of various ages and abilities. Standards require lifeguards to hold certificates in a lifesaving program, such as that offered by the Red Cross.

Racquet Sports Instructors

Accomplished players of the racquet sports often hold these positions. University training and certification is usually not necessary, although well-known players may receive preference in hiring, especially in fashionable, expensive clubs.

Diet/Nutrition Counselors

Health spas and upscale clubs may retain diet counselors with various backgrounds. Some may just be well versed on diet and nutrition from studying on their own. Others may have a more extensive background. A dietitian receives formal training at a university or nursing school and is registered or certified. A nutritionist is a person who has studied nutrition, either at a university or nursing school, and is registered or certified.

Masseurs and Masseuses

A good masseur or masseuse should have a thorough understanding of anatomy and physiology. Masseurs have usually studied massage in a school or acted as apprentices to licensed instructors. Some specialize in giving only facial massage; others are trained in Swedish massage, use of hydrotherapy, and other specialties. Licenses and certification are required in most states.

Spa and Locker Room Attendants

There are usually no requirements or experience necessary to become a spa or locker room attendant. Although the work will vary a great deal in different locales, some basic duties can be expected in most places. The attendant is responsible for seeing that the locker room and spa areas are clean and usable throughout the day. The attendant may also dispense toiletries, provide security to the area, and assist patrons as needed. This is an excellent job for the beginner who wants to learn about fitness careers. It is often possible to get a part-time job or a seasonal job so you can see where your interests lie.

Nursery/Child Care Attendants

Nursery attendants usually do not need a degree, although certification in the area of child development is helpful. An effective attendant enjoys children and keeps them clean, fed, and cared for while their parents are participating at the club. This is another good job for a person who wants to learn about the inside operations of a fitness center, spa, or health club. If you are interested in such a job for the summer, it is a good idea to apply to the director of the club several months in advance.

Sports Equipment Sales and Development

The expansion of interest in sports has resulted in an explosion of sports products, including sports equipment, sportswear, and sports novelties. Various types of employees are needed to develop, design, produce, and market these items. The fitness craze has resulted in a tremendous demand for exercise equipment. Shoes and special clothing exist for every conceivable type of athletic activity, and fads in sportswear change monthly.

If you enjoy sales, sporting goods sales may constitute a career option for you.

To prepare for such a role, college classes in business, marketing, or related areas can be helpful. Sales experience in other areas can also be useful in developing sales skills.

For more information contact:

Sporting Goods Manufacturers Association (SGMA)
200 Castlewood Dr.
North Palm Beach, FL 33408
sgma.com

10

STARTING YOUR OWN FITNESS OPERATION

WHILE THE PREVIOUS chapter reviewed various jobs in fitness centers and health clubs, another type of approach may be of interest to those who have an entrepreneurial spirit. Operating your own fitness center or similar operation can provide an assortment of challenges and opportunities.

Attracting Clients

An owner of a small fitness facility may know a lot about exercise, but very little about how to market and promote business. Most owners of studios understand the need for advertising in a highly competitive market, but many will go broke despite a good location and the ability to offer a quality class. The costs of professional advertising and promotion can be beyond your means, but you will save hundred of dollars if you take the time to make phone calls, write letters, and duplicate a few news releases yourself. These personal-touch endeavors can pay off tremendously and may bring even greater success than if you had had your advertisement prepared professionally.

Some marketing tips to help you promote your fitness business at a minimal cost are as follows:

1. First you must know your market and potential customers. What makes your studio unique in comparison to others within a five-mile radius? Why will clients want to attend your classes instead of another studio's classes? What is the average fitness level of your students, their age group, the proportion of women to men? Keep track of any changes in client type and number to understand why your market has shifted.

2. What type of client attends your classes? To know what media to target, you need to know what and whom your market is watching, listening to, and reading.

3. If you have newsworthy items to share with the public, broadcasting is an excellent media. Broadcast schedules may have spaces in their day for informative fitness bulletins. This also establishes your credibility in the community.

4. One of the best ways to draw attention to your studio is with an ad in your local yellow pages. Next, a news release should be sent to your local newspaper. This should be repeated every two to six months if there are updates you need to make the public aware of. For instance, if you are planning to sponsor a special program for an organization such as the American Heart Association, you should send news releases to all local newspapers and magazines. Spon-

soring new and different events is also an excellent promotional idea.

5. A good website can be invaluable. Available software makes it possible for anyone to create a simple site. Or you can obtain professional assistance. To keep costs down, consider hiring a college student or computer-savvy friend to help develop an effective Web presence.

6. The most important factor to keep in mind is that the business you are promoting is one that is needed by the public. If you're enthusiastic and believe in your studio, people will listen.

Developing News Releases

As the most basic sales vehicle, the news release features timely items for your studio. Even though all you write may not make it on the air or in print, in order for your news release to be read, you need to follow some simple guidelines. The first page of the news release should be brief and include only the most pertinent information. Be sure you have your name and title, organization name and address, telephone number, and E-mail address in the upper right-hand corner so that readers can contact you if necessary. At the top of the page, you also should type the release date, keeping it as current as possible. This can be followed by more detailed information. Using word processing software, type and double-space an original announcement on your own letterhead, making sure there are no errors.

In the first paragraph, you should include the complete name of the featured person, program, or organization. Then provide specific information about who the person is, or what the event is plus where and when it will take place.

In the second paragraph, underscore the importance of your featured person or organization with a significant fact. Then quote the most prominent person associated with the project; direct the quotation to the most significant readers. The quotation should attract their interest and cause them to pay closer attention to what they are reading. If you are targeting the release to a specific media source, introduce the name of the publication into this paragraph.

The third paragraph should give additional significant information about the person, organization, or event being featured. You can add here another noteworthy fact. If this release is about a person, you could add a quote that he or she made.

In the fourth paragraph, you can add information of interest to the public that you are attempting to attract, such as significant facts or a quotation by a known authority.

If you add further paragraphs, you may want to let your readers know what you want them to do as a result of reading your story. Include all information about how the reader can get involved. One of the main things to keep in mind is to just quote the facts as you know them.

The news release can be developed into a feature story to spark human interest on a broader scale. Therefore, ask your media sources if they would be interested in doing a feature story on your news item. You may generate enough interest for the editor to assign the story to one of the reporters. Send the news release to as many sources as possible. You can also post it on your website.

You may want to include photographs in your news release; just be sure to include the names of the people in the photos and to give credit to the photographer.

Keeping Clients

Now that you have attracted your clients, how do you keep them coming back? Here are some helpful hints:

1. Everyone loves personal attention to his or her specific needs. For instance, if you have older clients in your class that feel as though they are not keeping up with the younger ones, you might compliment them on their particular improvements. In addition, you should remind any beginning or special (overweight, medically impaired, and so forth) students to pace themselves and "listen to their body." Pacing means to exercise a little slower than the rest of the class. A person will do the same exercises, but may not go through as many repetitions. Your main point to the people in your class is that they should breathe as they exercise. Listening to one's body is always stressful in a class because everyone is an individual and not everyone can keep up the same pace. For instance, if someone has a bad back, there are certain exercises he or she should avoid. Another example would be an overweight person. You need to pay particular attention to overweight people because they are often so anxious to lose weight that they tend to overexercise. Overexercising in an overweight individual, or in any individual who enters your class in an unhealthy state, could lead to serious problems such as a heart attack. This is why we stress that you should have knowledge in cardiopulmonary resuscitation and first aid.

2. You may find that some of your clients love your class, but they cannot afford to attend as much as they would want to. In many parts of the country there is a system called bartering. To give an example, one person may have needlework or woodworking

skills. Another person may own chickens. The first person would barter with the second for some eggs by trading a pillow they embroidered or candlestick they made. You would be surprised how many interesting barters you can make with clients. You may find that you enjoy some of your "deals" more than what you would receive in money.

3. One of the best ways to keep clients coming back is to make your class an innovative one. This can be accomplished in many ways. One method is to have special deals available. For instance, if participants pay ahead for a month's worth of classes at three classes a week, you give them an extra free class each week. Another idea is to have prizes for the "one that breathed the best" or the "one who paced the best" or the "one who lost the most weight." The last suggestion, of course, would apply only to a special class in which many of your clients are striving for a similar goal, such as those who are attending Weight Watchers. A prize could be given to the person who wore the funniest T-shirt at your T-shirt contest class. Providing your students with a variety of music is always important. For special occasions, you could have a fifties rock 'n' roll theme. If participants dress with a fifties style, you could give a special prize. Many stores in your vicinity would love to give you coupons for a free yogurt, for example, to promote their product. So it's really not too difficult to obtain prizes for your students. Other prizes might be snazzy shoelaces, headbands, or socks. You may want to give a free class to a client who brings a new person into your classroom. You could also have a "free night." This is a great idea to introduce yourself to the community. Once the public experiences how much fun they can have in your class, they'll be coming back for more.

Owning a Studio

Owning your own studio can be very exciting, but also very demanding on your time. It is not unusual to spend up to fourteen hours a day at your business. Functions include offering classes to the public, teaching classes and other instructors, managing the business and employees, maintenance, and promotion and advertising of the studio.

Before considering opening your own business, it is advisable to have the experience of several years as a dance-exercise instructor and choreographer. You should have an understanding of exercise physiology and be trained and certified as a group-exercise instructor by a qualified organization. It also is desirable to have knowledge of business management, as this could determine the success or failure of your studio.

Start-up financing is a key consideration. Even for a small operation, you should have at least $20,000 to $30,000, or enough to cover your expenses for one full year. These costs will include rent, studio renovation, advertising and promotion, office supplies, mailing and copying costs, in addition to employees' salaries, accountants' fees, insurance, and lawyers. It may take at least a year or two before you start to make a profit. Keep in mind that many studios go out of business in six months due to the competition in the market at present, and you will need a period of time to become established, develop your program, and build up your clientele.

Choreography and Music Services

Choreography is the art of designing dance steps to music. Choreographing fitness activities can be fun, but it does require hours of preparation. The dilemma in creating a routine for an exercise program is to keep the abilities of your participants in mind. Some of them may be athletes, while others may be elderly, pregnant, or simply have "two left feet." If routines are not simplified and changed on a frequent basis, you may lose a class to frustration or boredom. A routine can easily be altered by changing arm movements or by lifting the spirits with new music, especially if the participants can sing along. Playing sing-along music is advantageous in that you can assess how participants are doing by seeing if they are able to talk to the persons near them, or if you notice them singing to the tune on the cassette player. In addition to making routines more enjoyable, exercising with music makes it easier to remember the steps to the routine and keeps the class together.

Listed here are several points to remember when you are the choreographer for a health fitness class:

1. Your sense of rhythm and timing is vital. You must always know where the beat of the music is and never lose it.

2. Choose a variety of music because everyone has a favorite type of music. Music is probably the best motivation for most students. If your exercise style tends more to jazz-type movements, your music should center on jazz/R&B /soul. If you tend more toward an athletic style, your music should probably lean toward harder rock and pop songs. Pop/country, soft rock, and old-time rock 'n' roll are good if you are teaching senior citizens, children, or a class with many types of individuals. In all cases, change your music frequently to avoid boredom.

3. In evaluating each song you choose, divide it into parts. Each part will have different sets of eight counts. Try to

keep the tune divided into no more than five parts and repeat the same movements when the music repeats itself. This simplifies the routine.

4. The energy and spirit of your music should match the energy and spirit of the exercises and steps you do and also should correspond with your style of teaching.

5. Once you have an outline of what you want to do, check the routine for smoothness of transitions. Also check for the correctness of body alignment. Make sure you are using both sides of the body to exercise the muscles more effectively.

6. Add arm movements to help the routine flow, stressing to the student the placement of the arm to work the arm muscles more effectively. During warm-up and cool down, the arm movements should be of lower intensity, while during peak time they should be of higher intensity.

If you wish to improve your routine or if you have never choreographed an exercise class, attend classes taught by highly recommended instructors. Observe not only the teacher, but also the people in the class. Is the spirit high and is the music motivating? Is everyone following the routine easily, in unison, and with good form? Are the transitions clean and do you like the teacher's style? Most importantly, was the whole body worked evenly from head to toe? When designing your program, make sure to reevaluate it periodically. Listen to your clients, and think about what they say. If they complain and drop out, there may be something you can do to improve the class. If they grow fit, and bring new clients to class, be sure you know what has been successful. The key to a good class is meeting the needs of your clients.

Third-party choreography and music services are available if you think what they offer is what you need for your class. Services offered include original music, choreography, videotapes, and voice programs. Keep in mind that an instructor has the right to ascertain precisely what he or she is buying from a music service. A legitimate organization should have absolutely no difficulty explaining from whom and in what manner its rights were obtained. Local music services are listed in the yellow pages under "aerobics" or "exercise and physical fitness programs."

In using music, don't overlook legal limitations. Many instructors prefer to make their own tapes for their classes, because they find that most records and tapes on the market are not appropriate to their routines or their clientele. Exercise instructors need to be aware, though, of the legal limits of taping popular music for dance exercise classes.

Under copyright law, the creator or owner of certain types of original musical compositions is afforded certain exclusive rights to exploit such works and certain concomitant protection against unauthorized persons doing so. There is no prohibition against or license required in connection with the performance of a sound recording itself. Therefore, if you just wanted to play the CD or commercially issued tape in an exercise class, without copying it, or if you were willing to record and use a "sound-alike" version, you would have to obtain a license from the publisher of the song but would not have to obtain permission from the music company. The license needed to record a musical composition, called a mechanical license, costs only a few cents per song per tape, and the performing license needed to play or otherwise perform the composition in class can generally be obtained inexpensively, frequently on an overall basis, from performing rights societies that represent music publishers in negotiating and collecting performance fees. The music services that manufacture and supply "sound-alike" recordings presumably have obtained the right to do so by securing the necessary mechanical and performing licenses from the applicable publishers. Thus, an individual facility or club could probably obtain the necessary performing licenses to permit the playing of musical compositions by means of unduplicated commercial recordings. It is advisable, for your own protection, to seek legal advice before choreographing your class.

Satellite Classes

In operating satellite classes, you basically operate your own business, but you don't own or rent the building that you use. You and those you hire teach at various locations like community centers, YMCAs, JCCs, health clubs, dance studios, and corporate centers. You manage the business aspect of your job in another facility, be it office space you rent or space you maintain in your own home. Your other duties include instructor training and choreography. Coordinating instructors and facilities can take up a lot of time. You can expect to work up to fourteen hours a day, six days a week, handling hiring, training, accounting, bookkeeping, program planning, and more.

To prepare for such a role, you should have experience as a group-exercise instructor and choreographer. You should have a working knowledge of anatomy and physiology with certification as a group-exercise instructor and in CPR. A course in business management is advisable. If one of your satellite programs is at a corporation or hospital for its employees, it is recommended that you have a bachelor's, master's, or doctoral degree in exercise physiology, kinesiology, or sports medicine, especially if you are going to be doing fitness testing.

Because you will be offering your classes in someone else's facility, you may find that the organization has particular goals in mind for which you may need to be prepared.

Corporate Exercise Programs

Top management support is essential before beginning a wellness program in a corporation, and it is critical to have this support continue for at least five years. The value of these programs must be understood by the major decision-makers in the company, so that the program's continuing life will be a priority in the overall management plan. Anything short of complete support will increase the possibility of lack of acceptance by employees or failure of the program for other reasons.

Interest in fitness programs among senior management may be created in a number of ways; one of the most effective is by showing them the results of cardiovascular risk evaluation questionnaires, self-administered by employees, which identify a significant number of individuals with a high risk of cardiovascular disease. Demonstrating the success of other fitness programs in other corporations may also be helpful.

The program goals must be realistic and specific. Such broad goals as "health care cost containment through individual health management" are difficult to measure or attribute to a fitness program. To be realistic, goals must have well-defined content and time periods. When specific goals and objectives that are consistent with corporate goals have been defined, the program can be designed. Personnel, facilities, and the program itself should be considered.

You must be able to communicate to employees the importance of physical fitness and to motivate individuals to participate. You should also be able to set an example by practicing a lifestyle of exercising regularly, either not using or being moderate in alcohol use, not smoking, and not being overweight. If this fitness profile is not maintained, the credibility of the program suffers.

Once top management support has been enlisted and a plan with appropriate personnel, facilities, and products has been designed, action must be taken to effectively implement the fitness program. Initially there should be an employee orientation to the program that presents the reasons for being fit and the potential benefits.

If the goals and objectives are clearly defined in terms of content and time duration, and if adequate, accurate, and timely data have been collected on the effects on the participants and the program costs, the next steps are to select the evaluator and the evaluation methods.

One approach to evaluation is for the sponsoring management, the fitness program director, and the participating employees to develop the evaluation methods at the time they define the goals and objectives of the program. Their involvement in this dynamic process will result in their understanding and making a commitment to the program components. As the goals and objectives are strengthened by periodic evaluation and the participants interact in a flexible format, the success of the process becomes evident.

Regardless of what other elements might be included in the planning of the health fitness program, the trend in business and industry is definitely toward expanding participation to include all levels of employees, rather than just executives. Also it is becoming accepted that, when possible, the program should be conducted on company time to increase motivation. At the least, employees should have a wide selection of possible times for participating.

Finally, it is a good idea to publish a regular newsletter to promote interest in the program. The newsletter (which in some cases can be published in electronic form to reduce printing and mailing costs) should publish schedules for use of facilities and upcoming classes as well as seminars and other group activities. It is also an excellent chance to increase health awareness through special columns written by experts on various subjects such as weight management, hypertension control, and stress reduction.

As for educational preparation, the corporation program director should have previous experience or specialized training in health fitness management and in data processing and statistical analysis. The fitness director must be experienced in the techniques of exercise testing and prescription and have knowledge of the physiological response to exercise and various stress testing protocols. Training in emergency procedures, including cardiopulmonary resuscitation and basic life support, is essential. Also specific experience or training in education or counseling is invaluable. These skills and experiences might be found among physicians, nurses, or those with special training in exercise physiology, physical education, or health fitness management.

Company physical fitness facilities vary in scope and cost. Facilities for an on-site program should provide, as a minimum, showers, locker rooms, and a meeting room for educational programs. The cost of a minimal on-site program is about $250 to $350 per participant per year. Companies may provide off-site fitness programs at the local YMCA or health club with the cost paid in full or shared with the employee. Some companies provide a health insurance premium deduction for employees who regularly attend the exercise program.

A comprehensive on-site program would provide rooms for stretching and aerobic dance classes as well as for stationary bicycles, treadmills, stair-climbing machines, weight-training equipment, bench presses, and leg equipment and abdominal machines, at the very least. Besides the equipment necessary for testing and exercise, computer support is essential for management and analysis.

Income Taxes

An unavoidable part of business operation is dealing with taxes. Taxes vary according to personal financial habits, state laws, and individual tax brackets. The guidelines below may help you to minimize tax payments.

Label a box, large manila envelope, or file drawer "taxes." There are also specially designed envelopes for this purpose, which can be found in any office products store. For each check or charge, be sure to include the amount, time, location, and business purpose of your expenditure. Make sure you get receipts for all your business-related purchases. Put all your receipts into this one place, and at the end of the year, you will have all your documentation together. Thus, it is important to be organized.

Keep an account book for jotting down all your various transactions that are business-related. A few minutes each day could save hours of frustration at the end of the year. Also consider purchasing tax software that can be used with any personal computer.

Deductions can be extensive and confusing. Consult a tax expert who will provide you with any necessary specific information. Business deductions you can use are education, travel, meals, and lodging (for example, attending a dance-exercise seminar). Other general business expenses you can deduct are supplies such as exercise mats, running shoes, tape recorders, and compact discs.

After you have calculated your business deductions, you now have your adjusted gross income. It is a financial plateau between certain deductions you are allowed to take. This figure is necessary to compute the second set of deductions that you are allowed by law.

Now that you know your adjusted gross income, you can list your next group of deductions. These deductions are called "itemized deductions," and they are subtracted from your adjusted gross income to arrive at your "taxable income." These items may include certain medical expenses, charitable contributions, and interest expenses. The tax rate depends on the individual and your personal situation.

The above material should help you become aware of how to prepare for reporting your tax situation. It is recommended, though, that professional consultation with a tax accountant or tax consultant be sought as the tax law is extensive and complex, and it is important to be accurate and complete in handling your records.

Insurance

Insurance is your business's protection. The moment you establish a business, you have also established the need for insurance. Fitness instructors need to protect themselves from potential liability claims, and you are particularly vulnerable to such claims if you own your own business.

Comprehensive general liability insurance protects individuals, professionals, and businesses from various liability hazards resulting from owned, leased, or otherwise occupied premises. With this insurance, the instructor of the class would have coverage for any injuries or damages if negligence were proven on her or his part.

Incidental professional liability insurance protects you from malpractice claims by any of your instructors, employees, or volunteers for bodily injury arising out of the performance of, or failure to perform, professional services. If an injury does occur, this coverage will protect you from an expensive lawsuit.

Additional named insurance coverage is especially important if you are teaching in a municipality, large commercial center, afterschool club, or a school district. It enables the landlords to be protected for their contingent liability for your acts.

Personal injury coverage protects you against suits involving slander, libel, and defamation of character, as well as false arrest and invasion of privacy. The coverage applies both to you and your employees. Below is a partial list of other types of coverage that may be equally important to you. The insurance industry is constantly creating new types of coverage. Find an experienced broker or agent to help you meet your needs.

Worker's compensation
Contractual liability
Fire/legal liability
Property insurance
Automobile insurance
Bonds

Major medical and
   hospitalization
Life insurance
Disability
Dental insurance
Accident insurance

Because the insurance needs of every business are specific, you will need to consult with a professional insurance service to ensure the most adequate and economical coverage for you.

11

OTHER SPORTS AND FITNESS–RELATED CAREERS

ALONG WITH THE careers profiled in previous chapters, a number of other occupations can be found within, or connected to, the general area of sports and fitness. Following is a brief look at some of them.

Public Relations and Sports Information Professionals

The public's hunger for information about their team, favorite player, or the next opponent must be satisfied. Those desires are met through the efforts of public relations personnel.

One of the most popular academic areas on campuses today is that of communications major. Within that broad subject field, one of the most exciting specialties involves sports.

The expansion of public relations extends to schools, colleges, sports organizations, and professional teams. PR people work to maintain a favorable opinion of their institutions. Those in sports work to obtain publicity to fill stadiums, increase the visibility of colleges, and promote players. The activities vary with the size of the college. For professional teams, the PR program will vary with the team level; major-league team agents will be busier than those at the lower levels. Another major factor that will affect this office's work is the success of the team and its players. Successful teams create great interest and consequently test the energies of the PR staff.

At the professional sports level, PR tasks might include coordinating public appearances by players, writing news releases or reports, assisting with charitable events, and making speeches; or working with senior citizens' organizations, jails, schools, community recreation programs, business and civic groups, hospitals, and others to promote the employing team or the sport in general.

Professional teams work closely with the news media on a daily basis to provide them with a wide variety of information. Often following a major trade, a firing, or the signing of a number one draft choice, PR people go into high gear as public interest reaches a frenzy. However, even the daily schedules are hectic.

In many cases, sports publicity people for professional teams come from sports staffs of newspapers or from college campuses where they served as sports information directors. These individuals know how to work with the media and the public they serve.

At the college level, the public relations specialist for athletics is called the Sports Information Director (SID) or Director, Media Relations for Athletics. Large universities may have three or more professionals, a few secretaries, and many student assistants. Small colleges, on the other hand, may have only a part-time SID (or none at all).

Here are some of the typical activities of sports publicists at the college and professional levels:

- Establish excellent interpersonal relationships with athletic and school administrators, coaching staff and players, and print and electronic journalists.
- Prepare media guides that contain information on each player and the team and that may also contain statistics and records for the sport. At the professional level, a team yearbook is produced.
- Organize press briefings with newspaper writers and TV and radio reporters to bring them information about a player or a team.
- Arrange press conferences for the coach and/or players.
- Send news releases—usually a couple of pages worth of any new information—to the media (newspapers, radio, and TV).
- Send specific news releases, for example, to provide information to a player's hometown newspaper.
- Maintain files of historical and statistical data on athletes and teams.
- Direct the press box for certain sports; that is, arrange for seating and materials for newspaper, radio, and television people, as well as for distribution of admission credentials.
- Maintain a scrapbook of clipped newspaper items about the team(s) and players.
- Arrange for photographs of each player (head and shoulders) to be taken as well as action team photos and film (color for TV). Films and photographs are made available to the media.

- Answer requests for information to the league office, other teams, and to the general public.
- Write stories, because not all newspapers can send a reporter to cover an event; therefore, a story often is written and distributed by the sports publicist.
- Engage in professional development and growth through conferences, meetings, and readings concerning innovations and changes (cable television, endorsements, and National Collegiate Athletic Association and National Association for Intercollegiate Athletics regulations, and so forth).

Preparation for this career involves completing college courses in writing, computers, television, public speaking, journalism, and photography. Although a few opportunities may exist for high school graduates who show very special ability or expertise (such as in photography or video), college-level preparation is normally expected. A college major in communications with an emphasis in journalism and/or radio-TV, along with electives in public relations and physical education, will provide an excellent background. Also, if available, take an elective in sport studies, such as a course in Sports and Society or the History of Sports.

Try to obtain a position as an intern or part-time student aide in the sports information office; if that is not possible, valuable alternatives are student newspaper work, playing a sport, or working for the college radio station, newspaper, yearbook, or television station.

Sports Photographers

Want to be close to the sports excitement? Consider photographing sporting events.

Sports photographers capture on film some of the beauty of sports. A good sports photographer possesses excellent skills developed through many years of experience. If this sounds too demanding, consider beginning your career by "shooting" an amateur competition with a simple photographic camera or an inexpensive cartridge motion picture or video camera. If your interest develops, purchase more sophisticated equipment. Many local newspapers and school yearbooks need photographs; ask them if they would like some of yours. You may even be paid! Many schools film and videotape athletic events for students, players, and coaches to review. This may be an opportunity to gain some experience while aiding the school.

Some photographers work for specific magazines or newspapers. If these are general publications, the photography staff will cover subjects other than sports; although a few photographers may specialize in athletics, they may be called to work on other assignments. Naturally, those employed by sports magazines or newspapers would only work in athletics.

A significant number of photographers in this field work as freelancers. This means they are self-employed and work for a number of publications. Some will receive specific assignments to cover particular events and will sell the "shots" they take. Others will work part-time for a couple of newspapers, supplying them with several photographs a week. Still others may attend games and hope they will get some photos of a spectacular event to sell to a magazine or newspaper.

Agents and Sports Representatives

In this era of fantastic salaries for professional athletes, the agent has become a visible member of the sports scene. Agents, sometimes called representatives, act as the players' intermediaries with the team's owner and general manager to secure the best financial and playing arrangement for the athlete. The use of agents occurs in several professions: for example, writers use literary agents and those in show business use booking agents.

Agents are usually lawyers or accountants. They obtain their salary as a percentage of the income the player will receive from the team (or athletic event, as in boxing) and other monetary deals, such as endorsements. Agents normally receive 10 percent for their negotiation of the contract. When one considers the earnings of today's athletes, many of whom draw multimillion-dollar annual salaries, you realize that this sports career provides an excellent salary.

In addition to negotiating contracts, many serve as financial agents for players, making suggestions for investments, product endorsements, and handling income taxes. Some act as representatives for organizations such as those for football players or for baseball umpires. In doing so, they work to obtain better salaries, retirement benefits, and improved working conditions.

Successful professionals in this field believe they play an important role in negotiating contracts. They may lend objectivity to a situation, because the player or management may not be able to evaluate the athlete's contribution to the team—that is, the player's bargaining position. They also serve their clients through careful examination of the language of a contract, for example, the wording of no-cut clauses. Following the signing, as the contract goes into effect, agents may keep their clients informed on legal developments, such as the free agent rule; they may become involved if a contract breach occurs.

Opportunities for agents in the future will remain small in number, but the salaries will continue to be excellent. If you're interested, the best background is law or accounting. For law, this means four years of college in which you must do well academically, and then three years of law school. Accounting will normally require completing a bachelor's degree. While in school, association with sports as a player, writer, or broadcaster will provide excellent experience.

Sports Facility Maintenance Personnel

Long before players and fans arrive, the ground crew prepares the fields and arenas for athletic contests not only for games and events, but also for practice.

Sometimes this requires hard work into the early hours of the morning at the busier locations. For example, at New York's Madison Square Garden, the following may happen in twenty-four hours: an afternoon circus performance, a hockey game that evening, and basketball practice the following morning! At the other end of the spectrum, college stadium or community field maintenance proceeds in a much more leisurely fashion.

Most employees in these positions learn their skills on the job. However, some positions—involving things such as maintaining grass playing fields, equipment, and supervision of employees—require specific knowledge. These individuals may have a degree in recreation or sports management. Opportunities exist in a variety of situations; each town, city, school, college, and professional team has an athletic facility that needs constant maintenance. If you have an interest in a particular sport (soccer, hockey, lacrosse), you may need to move to pursue it as certain sports are played on a regional basis only.

Stadium and Arena Concessionaires

One of the most lucrative sports-related occupations involves owning a concession. Generally, concessions sell everything from hats to peanuts and have little competition.

Although few opportunities exist for obtaining a concession stand, some may be available at colleges; these go out for bid from time to time. To obtain a position as vendor, call a local college or professional team. Most likely, the procedure will involve going to the office of the concessionaire and filling out appropriate forms. You may wish to consider becoming a vendor part-time; this job will gain you free admission to the events and enable you to obtain money for saving and spending. It's difficult and hard work carrying boxes around for several hours, many times in hot temperatures, while hawking your wares, but in addition to your salary, you learn patience and hard work.

Previously employed persons receive preference; as those persons leave, others are called. The first to sign up are first called. Sometimes you can get your start when extra personnel are added for big games—those in which attendance will be greater than usual.

Believe it or not, some professional players originally worked selling in the stands before making it big on the playing field. Although this might not be the best way to make it in the pros, it does permit the opportunity to be close to a sport you love.

Sports Instructors

In addition to general fitness instructors, those who teach skills in specific sports also play important roles. They cover areas such as golf, tennis, SCUBA diving, swimming, martial arts, and hiking.

Frequently called "pros," they teach individuals and small groups everything from a general introduction to the activity to its finer points.

Many such sports pros have had successful careers and some have developed a following. Several continue to compete, if only regionally, using teaching to supplement their income during the off season. Instructors often are employed by sports facilities such as golf, swimming, or country clubs; some own a "pro shop," which sells sporting equipment. In some cases, they own their own schools and conduct courses there and in the community. For example, a SCUBA diver, skater, or gymnast, in addition to offering classes at her or his school, will offer courses at the local evening school and community college certain nights of the week.

In preparing for a career in this area, school courses in business, communication arts, and understanding others (history and the social sciences) will provide a good academic background. This must be combined with sports involvement, preferably as a participant. It may be possible in certain areas, such as swimming, not to have been a well-known athlete, but to have served as a successful coach. Although college is not always necessary, it will be helpful. Salaries vary dramatically with the instructors' success and reputation. Those who have authored a popular book, for example, may be frequently quoted in newspapers or generally have a celebrity status and receive excellent salaries for tutoring individuals or consulting with teams.

Statisticians

Statistics no longer exist just for "sports trivia fans." Coaches have expanded their interest in this area. The computer has emerged as a weapon in their arsenal. The data supplied by the computer add to the coach's knowledge of her or his team or of the opposing team, providing information that can assist with decision making. For example, the computer can process a great deal of data and find patterns. Football scouts can provide the computer with statistics on an opposing team and then program it to provide information such as what play the team tends to run in a given situation; for example, when losing in the fourth quarter, the opposing team has a tendency to pass to the tight end on third down.

Statistics are kept at most levels of play. Which information is kept depends for the most part upon the philosophy of the coach. Using basketball as an example, one coach may only want rebounding statistics on her or his players; another may keep shot charts (location of shots taken) and turnovers (how many and which players lost the ball to the other team); and still another might keep vast amounts of information on his or her team and others. This may include such detailed information in a scouting report as the number of passes made between each player during a basketball game. Many high school coaches record extra statistics, those over and above the information kept by the official scorer.

The coach at this level can be greatly aided by a competent student statistician; likewise the student can gain valuable experience. Normally the coach will have a prepared form on which to record the information. The coach will explain the procedures to be followed and will allow the aspiring statistician to gain some experience in intra-squad and preseason scrimmages. Once the season begins, the coach will expect perfect accuracy. College students may wish to approach a coach at their school about aiding a team with statistics. Experience will prove helpful. If you lack the background, you may wish to practice taking "stats" when watching a game or event. Although this is quite minimal, it might convince a coach of your desire to serve as a statistician. Knowledge of personal computers, data entry, and programming will prove beneficial.

Careers as sports statisticians remain quite limited on a full-time basis; however, several opportunities do exist to follow this job as an avocation. It should be mentioned that developing some skill in this area would prove beneficial in related areas such as sports information and newspaper careers.

Scouts

Scouts' decisions affect players, coaches, and games more than most people realize. They are sports intelligence agents. Scouting takes two forms: evaluating potential players and studying future opponents.

At the college level, players are chosen to fill the ranks of the team. Consequently, college coaches (even at small colleges) continually assess high school athletes; those of exceptional ability are offered scholarships. The selection of the correct person contributes to team success. Inability to make the appropriate selection may result in the firing of the coach. College scouts attend high school games, read magazines and newspapers, and get letters from alumni. To identify potential players, the real talent comes in judging which will truly become stars or superstars. Usually an assistant is designated to serve as a head scout; some freelance scouts exist. These aid colleges by providing individual reports to specific coaches and general publications evaluating players' abilities.

Another area of scouting involves observing opponents' teams to prepare to play them. In this case, the scout records the system used and players' abilities and tendencies; specific details are extremely important. The information obtained forms the basis of the scouting report distributed to the coaching staff and team. Again, the school's coaches perform most of this work. However, some individuals and small companies do scouting on an independent basis.

At the professional level, scouting follows a similar structure but is of an even more serious nature. Many teams employ scores of full-time and part-time scouts.

Often most teams know of the "blue-chip" player; therefore, the real test of a scout is to locate the "sleeper," the late-blooming player who, with proper coaching, will develop into the superstar. It is the sleeper player who must be kept a secret. Some scouts believe that scouting is like any other kind of espionage: if your secrets aren't airtight, you're out of business.

Great time and effort typically go into the scout's work in measuring opposing teams and preparing game plans. Films and videotapes provide the opportunity to carefully scrutinize the opposition.

More opportunities exist for scouting positions in professional sports than in college ranks. The job would involve employment with a team or scouting organization.

Preparation for scouting careers at any level involves expert knowledge of physical and psychological ability. Most scouts are former players and coaches. Salaries are good to very good, but for most, part of the reward is knowing that they located another superstar.

Sports Academicians

In addition to college instructors who teach courses in professional areas (physical education, sports management, physical therapy), the expansion of programs related to sports studies, sports health sciences, and related courses on college campuses has created a need for expanded faculty.

In recent years, several scholars have begun to examine various aspects of sports from the perspective of their academic areas of study. These individuals have approached athletics and organized sports in systematic ways, armed with an excellent knowledge of how to conduct in-depth studies of a particular topic. In addition, they prepare courses of study for teaching.

Sports historians examine areas such as the biographies of famous athletes or trends from past decades, such as the origin of a sport. They also work to encourage high school teachers to incorporate athletics into their courses when teaching U.S. history. Frequently, these individuals publish articles in the journals for the appreciation of the reader and the expansion of knowledge.

Some sociologists have studied the role of sports in society. For example, they investigate topics such as racial problems, attitudes toward winning and losing, and the effect money has had upon athletes. Like other academic persons, most sociologists teach in colleges. Those with a special interest in athletics frequently offer courses with titles such as Sociology of Sport and Sport in American Society.

Running therapy, mental toughness, and the psychology of coaching are some of the topics of interest to sport psychologists. These individuals have a particular interest in the mental aspects of athletics. Frequently they provide guidance to players and coaches concerning how they can achieve greater success through closer attention to the psychological aspects of athletics. For coaches this means subjects such as motivation and the establishment of smooth working relationships with players; for players it means areas such as mental aspects of relaxation and of pre-game preparation.

Most jobs in the area of sports academics exist at the university level. This means that if you have an interest in this area, you will need to attend graduate school and obtain a doctorate. A love of reading and scholarly activity is important, as well as an ongoing desire to add to the body of knowledge of sports. Interested? Perhaps someday you may teach a course entitled "The Contribution of Athletics to American Culture" or "Management Techniques for Sports Facilities." Or maybe you'll conduct research on "Mental Aspects of Pre-Game Preparation" or "The Value of Sports in a Small Town."

Equipment Managers

For those without a college degree, one job possibility is taking care of players' and teams' equipment.

The person responsible for the handling and care of everything from bats to helmets is the equipment manager. This profession offers opportunities for employment largely at the college and professional levels. The equipment manager has the responsibility of keeping the team's equipment cleaned and in good repair, having the equipment available for practice and games (this means traveling with the team), and providing security for the equipment. The last serves as the greatest problem of the equipment manager. At the professional level, this person is often aided by an assistant; at the college level, by the team's student managers. The assistant or student manager may help the team with other tasks, as necessary, too.

Persons employed in this profession normally have a great interest in the sport with which they are associated; often they have played or coached. Some have served as salespersons of sports equipment. No special training or education is necessary, but knowledge of the equipment and the ability to perform minor repairs is important. Also, the personal qualities of reliability and punctuality are a must.

APPENDIX A

Selected Sports and Fitness–Related Organizations

THE FOLLOWING ORGANIZATIONS can offer a variety of helpful information. Many will be able to provide requirements for certain jobs, details on educational opportunities, and additional sources of information you may desire. These are listed in alphabetical order by association name.

Aerobics and Fitness Association of America
15250 Ventura Blvd, Ste. 200
Sherman Oaks, CA 91403
afaa.com

American Academy of Physical Medicine and Rehabilitation
One IBM Plaza, Ste. 2500
Chicago, IL 60611-3604
aapmr.org

American Academy of Physical Therapy
3600 General Meyer Ave., Ste. A
New Orleans, LA 70114
aaptnet.org

American Alliance for Health, Physical Education, Recreation
and Dance
1900 Association Dr.
Reston, VA 20191-1598
aahperd.org

American Association of Personal Trainers
P.O. Box 11177
Newport Beach, CA 92658
aapt.net

American College of Sports Medicine
P.O. Box 1440
Indianapolis, IN 46206-1440
acsm.org

American Council on Exercise
4851 Paramount Dr.
San Diego, CA 92123
acefitness.org

American Fitness Professionals & Associates
P.O. Box 214
Ship Bottom, NJ 08008
sfpafitness.com

American Occupational Therapy Association
4720 Montgomery La.
P.O. Box 31220
Bethesda, MD 20824-1220
aota.org

American Physical Therapy Association
1111 N. Fairfax St.
Alexandria, VA 22314-1488
apta.org

American Society of Exercise Physiologists
c/o College of St. Scholastica
Dept. of Exercise Physiology
1200 Kenwood Ave.
Duluth, MN 55811
css.edu

American Therapeutic Recreation Association
1414 Prince St., Ste. 204
Alexandria, VA 22314
atra-tr.org

American Yoga Association
P.O. Box 19986
Sarasota, FL 34276
americanyogaassociation.org

Association for Supervision and Curriculum Development
1703 N. Beauregard St.
Alexandria, VA 22311-1714
acsd.org

Association for Worksite Health Promotion
60 Revere Dr., Ste. 500
Northbrook, IL 60062
ahp7.org

Canadian Association of Fitness Professionals
2851 John St.
P.O. Box 42011
Markham, ON
Canada L3R 5R7
canfitpro.com

Canadian Association for Health, Physical Education,
    Recreation and Dance
2197 Riverside Dr., Ste. 403
Ottawa, ON
Canada K1H 7X3
cahperd.ca

Canadian Association of Occupational Therapists
CTTC Bldg., Ste. 3400
1125 Colonel By Dr.
Ottawa, ON
Canada K1S 5R1
caot.ca

Canadian Football Players Association
603 Argus Rd., Ste. 207
Oakville, ON
Canada L6J 6G6
cflpa.com

Canadian Kinesiology Alliance
Alliance Canadienne de Kinésiologie
6519-B Mississauga Rd.
Mississauga, ON
Canada L5N 1A6
cka.ca

Canadian Physiotherapy Association
2345 Yonge St., Ste. 410
Toronto, ON
Canada M4P 2E5
physiotherapy.ca

Coaching Association of Canada
141 Laurier Ave. West, Ste. 300
Ottawa, ON
Canada K1P 5J3
coach.ca

Major League Baseball Players Association
12 E. 49th St., 24th Fl.
New York, NY 10017
bigleaguers.yahoo.com

National Alliance for Youth Sports
2050 Vista Pkwy.
West Palm Beach, FL 33411
nays.org

National Association of Basketball Coaches
9300 W. 110th St., Ste. 640
Overland Park, KS 66210
nabc.ocsn.com

National Association of Sports Officials
2017 Lathrop Ave.
Racine, WI 53405
naso.org

National Athletic Trainers' Association
2952 Stemmons Freeway
Dallas, TX 75247-6916
nata.org

National Collegiate Athletic Association
700 W. Washington St.
P.O. Box 6222
Indianapolis, IN 46206-6222
ncaa.org

National Council for Therapeutic Recreation Certification
7 Elmwood Dr.
New City, NY 10956
nctrc.org

National Endurance Sports Trainers Association
31441 Santa Margarita Pkwy., Ste. A-140
Rancho Santa Margarita, CA 92688-1835
nestacertified.com

National High School Athletic Coaches Association
P.O. Box 4342
Hamden, CT 06514
hscoaches.org

National Junior College Athletic Association
P.O. Box 7305
Colorado Springs, CO 80933-7305
njcaa.org

National Therapeutic Recreation Society
22377 Belmont Ridge Rd.
Ashburn, VA 20148
nrrsnrpa.com

President's Council on Physical Fitness and Sports
Dept. W
200 Independence Ave. SW, Rm. 738-H
Washington, DC 20201-0004
fitness.gov

Women's Basketball Coaching Association
4646 Lawrenceville Hwy.
Lilburn, GA 30047-3620
wbca.org

Appendix B

Exercise Dos and Don'ts

WHAT DANGER CAN occur from improper exercise technique? Plenty. The main threat is injury to the lower back and knees. Incorrect or quick, uncontrolled movement can compress the back and strain the knees. Exercise benefits can be sabotaged when specific muscle groups are not worked effectively.

The following steps can be used in guiding students toward executing proper technique during exercise.

1. Make sure initial posture position is correct before beginning to move.
2. The body must stay balanced throughout the movement and should continue to be aligned, especially at the knees and pelvis. The knees always bend over the toes, and there should be no hyperextension of the back.
3. Relax all body parts not specifically involved in the exercise. This reduces muscular tension and conserves energy.

4. Don't jump side-to-side on one foot. This may cause torn ligaments or fractures.
5. Don't jump so high that both feet are more than six inches off the ground at the same time. The shock of landing increases the risk of injury.
6. Remember to breathe! During stretching, breathe in and out, rhythmically. For example, when stretching up, breathe in. When bending over, breathe out.
7. Stretching should follow a period of walking around a little to get the body warmed up. Warm muscles stretch 30 percent more than cold muscles. A cold muscle, due to its limited performance abilities, can easily be damaged.
8. During stretching, never bounce or make jerky movements. Stretching should always be slow and easy.
9. Avoid too many continuous movements of any body part, as this burns off all the glycogen (carbohydrates) and causes the accumulation of lactic acid (waste product), which leads to an anaerobic state (lack of oxygen).
10. During the five to ten minutes of peak exercise, participants' heart rates should reach 80 percent of their age-specific maximums.
11. Never do aerobics in bare feet.

Make sure your program is progressive. It should be one that challenges participants of every skill level without demanding too much of beginners. Instructors should encourage students to build up to the full routine gradually. Flexibility, endurance, strength, and muscle tone will come, but they take time. When students feel they've reached their limits, instructors should not pressure them to do more.

Appendix C

Teaching Guidelines for the Multilevel Class

TEACHING IN FITNESS-RELATED areas sometimes involves dealing with students of various levels of fitness within a single class. Below are helpful guidelines to help you avoid the common pitfalls of a multilevel class.

1. Obtain written permission from any student (or his or her parent or guardian if student is a minor) who has a medical problem before allowing her or him to participate in your class.
2. Always give a review of the class format, stressing a non-competitive atmosphere.
3. Remind participants during sessions to "listen to their bodies."
4. Give students specific instructions on how to pace themselves and breathe and move properly.

5. Easily fatigued beginning exercise students need constant encouragement, especially so they do not feel they cannot keep up with others.
6. A person who is overweight or has low self-esteem should be treated sensitively and given lots of motivation, support, and reassurance.
7. Some intermediate students go overboard and others barely push themselves. Your responsibility is to assist each one to reach her or his highest training level without injury while improving self-esteem. Offer them hand or leg weights, if appropriate, to enhance cardiovascular output.
8. The advanced students, who are often bored in an intermediate class, can be further stimulated by periodically offering them advice and means toward improving body alignment and control with each movement.
9. Advanced students should be instructed to rest a day between strenuous workouts. This group tends toward a high level of injuries due to overuse of the body.
10. Exercise in front of your students until many are familiar with the routines. Eliminate boredom by having an intermediate or advanced student lead a routine. This will permit you the time to circulate through your class, motivating, adjusting, and encouraging your participants.
11. If you are unable to leave the front of the room, make eye contact with students who need your attention to encourage or pace them.

Further Reading

Arnheim, Daniel, and William Prentice. *Principles of Athletic Training*. St. Louis: Mosby Year Book, 1996.

Benton, Debra, and D. A. Benton. *Secrets of a CEO Coach*. New York: McGraw-Hill, 1999.

Clover, Jim. *Sports Medicine Essentials*. Orange, Calif.: Career Publishing, 2001.

Collison, Jim. *NO-How Coaching*. Dulles, Va.: Capital Books, 2001.

Heitzmann, W. R. *Careers for Sports Nuts and Other Athletic Types*. Chicago: VGM Career Books, 1997.

Johnson, Harry. *Standing the Gaff: The Life and Hard Times of a Minor League Umpire*. Lincoln: University of Nebraska Press, 1994.

Karlin, Len. *The Guide to Careers in Sports*. E. M. Guild, 1996.

McGovern, Michael. *The Encyclopedia of Twentieth Century Athletes*. New York: Facts on File, 2001.

Nagle, Jeanne. *Careers in Coaching*. New York: Rosen Publishing Group, 2000.

————. *Choosing a Career as a Coach*. New York: Rosen Publishing Group, 2001.

Roberts, Robin. *Careers for Women Who Love Sports*. Brookfield, Conn.: Millbrook Press, 2000.

Still, Bob, and Jeffrey Stern. *101 Tips for Youth Sports Officials*. Racine, Wis.: Referee Enterprises, 2000.

Voeller, Edward. *Athletic Trainer*. Mankato, Minn.: Capstone Press, 2000.

Weinburg, Robert. *Psychology of Officiating*. Champaign, Ill.: Human Kinetics, 1995.

Wilson, Robert. *Careers in Sports, Fitness, and Recreation*. Hauppauge, N.Y.: Barron's Educational Series, 2001.

Wuest, Deborah, and Charles Bucher. *Foundations of Physical Education and Sport*. New York: McGraw-Hill, 1999.

About the Author

Ray Heitzmann, a faculty member at Villanova University, has taught and coached successfully in New Jersey, Pennsylvania, Illinois, and New York at the high school and college levels. Formerly he taught in the College of Allied Health Sciences at Thomas Jefferson University. His specialties in coaching include development of fundamental skills, performance enhancement, strategy and tactics, and sports literature. During the 1980s his interest in women's sports greatly expanded; the 1990s found him coaching women's AAU basketball. His flag football team won the Philadelphia area college championship and participated in the National Women's Flag Football Championship.

Ray has written a variety of articles on sports and athletics; some have appeared in *Coach and Athlete, Illinois Libraries, The Beachcomber, Coaching Clinic, Catholic Library World, PhillySport,* the *Philadelphia Inquirer,* the *National Association of Basketball Coaches Bulletin,* and others. He has appeared frequently on radio and television shows discussing sports careers, academics and athletics, and sports in society.

In the area of career education he has worked with groups of school students, taught in-service courses for educators, spoken at conferences, and published articles in *Real World, Career World,* the *California Social Studies Review,* and others. His *Opportunities in Marine and Maritime Careers* and *Careers for Sports Nuts and Other Athletic Types* have been published by VGM Career Books, a division of the McGraw-Hill companies.

In the wonderful world of sports, in addition to playing and coaching, he has had the good fortune to serve as a sportswriter, guest commentator on professional wrestling and basketball, umpire, referee, and fan, and he gladly admits loving them all.